EVERYDAY PUBLIC RELATIONS FOR LAWYERS

GINA FURIA RUBEL, ESQ.

First published in 2007

Furia Rubel Communications, Inc.
P.O. Box 348
Fountainville, PA 18923
United States of America

www.ThePRLawyer.com / www.FuriaRubel.com

ISBN: 978-0-9801719-0-7

Library of Congress Control Number: 2007941911

Edited by Jennifer Batchelor, Esq., Batchelor Media LLC
Proofread by Barbara McIntosh Webb, Esq.
Art direction and cover design by Alexis Doyle, Kitsune Graphic Design
Illustration by Pat Achilles, AchillesCards.com
Interior design and layout by Kitty Mace, Origin Creative Services, OriginOnline.com

Printed by United Book Press, Inc.
Printed in the United States of America.

"Attorneys who advertise usually look like ambulance chasers. On the other hand, attorneys who know how to use PR can look like stars. Simply put, Gina's book is the best I've seen for attorneys on public relations."

—**Michael Port, Author of**
Book Yourself Solid **and** *Beyond Booked Solid*

"*Everyday Public Relations for Lawyers* is filled with practical PR strategies, models, and success tips that will enhance your professional image and improve communications with the media, your community and your clients."

—**Priscilla Y. Huff, Author of** *Make Your Business Survive and Thrive!: 100+ Proven Marketing Methods...*

"Two bright lawyers, equally skilled. Lawyer A has a national reputation and an enormous, ongoing stream of the most interesting business; Lawyer B ekes out a living. Lawyer B should have bought Gina's book."

—**Ross Fishman, Esq., President,
Ross Fishman Marketing, Inc.**

"Every attorney I know should read this book. Gina's practical tips and guidance offer everything an attorney needs to know about public relations and how to use it strategically to get results."

—**Joseph P. Stampone, Esq., Founding Shareholder,
Stampone D'Angelo Renzi DiPiero, P.C.**

"While many lawyers are great practitioners in the courtroom, they fail miserably when attempting to promote themselves, their firms and their clients in the media. Gina's book is a step-by-step, easy-to-read compendium of public relations do's and don'ts for lawyers. It should be a gift to every law school graduate."

—Sayde J. Ladov, Esq., Abrahams, Loewenstein & Bushman
(2009 Philadelphia Bar Association Chancellor)

"This exceptional resource should be in every law firm across the world. Any lawyer serious about growing their book of business must read and apply all of Gina's recommended practical strategies from this book! This all-in-one guide is jam-packed with information on the what, why and how of public relations for lawyers. Not only will attorneys boost their reputation and generate buzz in the media, they will double their productivity. From the traditional practices to Web 2.0—*Everyday Public Relations* has it all."

—Neen James, International Productivity Expert
and Author of *Secrets of Super-Productivity*

"Gina has done a great service to the legal profession—and the media—with this sensible and comprehensive book. I highly recommend it to lawyers as well as PR and marketing professionals entering the legal market."

—Rich Klein, President, Riverside Public Relations LLC

"This insightful guide provides a treasure trove of great advice in a style that is fun to read. Gina's background as a lawyer turned public relations professional gives her a unique perspective on lawyer rainmaking. Her chapter on Internet networking is a fascinating orientation to developing opportunities. I highly recommend this book to lawyers at all stages of their careers."

—Rudolph Garcia, Esq., Buchanan Ingersoll & Rooney PC

"As a business owner who handles her own PR, I found this book extremely informative and helpful. I'm sure both lawyers and self-employed people in a myriad of industries will find it easy to read and understand and will come away revved up about trying some of these strategies and tactics themselves."

—**Gayle Crist Shisler, Life Coach, HealthyLife Planning**

"Gina has condensed her years of public relations experience into a systematic, step-by-step approach that would benefit any lawyer who interacts with the public, the media and other lawyers."

—**Jason P. Lisi, Esq., President, Legal Internet Solutions Incorporated**

Gina's insight into public relations is straightforward and understandable. Her book provides valuable content and a practical approach to reaching a targeted audience. Lawyers, legal marketing professionals, and other service providers interested in raising awareness in the marketplace will find it required reading for developing and implementing a successful public relations plan.

—**Laura Powers, President, Harvest Graphics**

"Gina writes with great clarity and creativity. Public relations is a difficult concept for many lawyers to grasp and understand. Gina's book peels away the layers of the complex issue of PR and provides simple but strategic advice. I'll keep the guide in my office and recommend that the lawyers in my firm do the same."

—**Robin M. Nolan, Director of Marketing, White and Williams LLP**

"Keep *Everyday Public Relations for Lawyers* on your desk for handy reference to create effective promotions and lasting impressions. It contains exactly the type of strategies law firms need to support their business development programs and increase their books of business."

—**Susan Williams, President & CEO, S.A.W. Broadcasting, Inc.**

"Every lawyer should refer to *Everyday Public Relations for Lawyers* every day. It's practical, informative and to the point. If more lawyers applied the strategies in this book, they would improve their media relationships overnight."

—Karen Friedman, President, Karen Friedman Enterprises, Inc.,
and Author of *Speaking of Success*

"Gina combines her background as a lawyer with her excellent communication skills and a strong dose of common sense to provide practical advice to other lawyers."

—Molly Peckman, Esq., Monthly Columnist, *The Legal Intelligencer*

"The jury has returned their verdict, and it's a win-win for Gina Furia Rubel. Her expertise as a practicing attorney and public relations specialist come together perfectly in this easy-to-read, step-by-step guide, a must-have for any lawyer hoping to expand the boundaries of their professional profile."

—Debora Russo Haines, Esq.

"When I need legal analysis for a story I'm working on, I call a lawyer and I know that lawyer will be prepared for the interview if they take the advice that Gina Furia Rubel provides for them in her book."

—Brad Segall, Suburban Bureau Chief, KYW Newsradio and
Host "The Philadelphia Agenda" on WOGL-FM

"A manual all attorneys should keep at their fingertips! Gina provides a comprehensive approach to building and implementing a sound public relations strategy in an easily consumable fashion. A good read before undertaking any serious public relations efforts."

—M. Toni Buckley, Senior Management Consultant
to Top PR Firms and Fortune 40, 100 and 500 Companies Worldwide

"Gina Furia Rubel's book demystifies the art of public relations for the legal profession. The plain-language strategies, insights and practical tips in this solid reference are indispensable to any attorney seeking to build a practice."
—Mark A. Tarasiewicz, Chairman, Philadelphia Public Relations Association

"Gina combines the training and good judgment of an attorney with the experience and creativity of a seasoned public relations professional to produce a valuable guide loaded with practical and insightful tips for every lawyer. Gina has a passion for her work and it shows!"
—Daniel A. Cirucci, Lecturer in
Corporate Communications, Penn State University

"This is the ultimate 'how to' public relations book for law firms. This is a must-read if you want to take your business to another level."
—Chuck Polin, President, The Training Resource Group

I dedicate this book to my husband, Scott, and our two amazing children, Gianna and Ford—I thank God for you!

To Marc Antony—I remember you always with love.

ACKNOWLEDGEMENTS

To the WONDERFUL people in my life…

Writing a book has been a dream of mine since I was a child. I always thought my first would be a children's book. But for the past five years I have been talking about writing a public relations guide for lawyers. I've had ideas, thoughts, goals and a purpose for writing the book but always said to myself and others, "I'll get to it as soon as I have time."

Well, folks, as my dear friend and colleague Neen James said, "Gina, you will only have time if you make time." Neen urged me to set aside just 15 minutes a day. She showed me how to organize my thoughts and stay on track, and she checked in to make sure I was doing what I said I'd do, "make time." It is to Neen that I owe a huge debt of gratitude—otherwise, I think I'd still be saying, "I will," rather than, "I have." So to Neen I say thank you my dear friend. You're a true productivity guru and inspiration.

I've also always said that I want to work with people who are smarter than I am. I want to be inspired and challenged. Call it luck. Call it God's good graces. Call it what you will, but if you ask for it, I believe the Universe will provide. I am so blessed to be surrounded by amazing people in life and in business.

To my confidant and spiritual guide, Cheyenne, thank you for listening, understanding and always sending light.

To my editor, Jennifer Batchelor, it's been a long road but a smooth one because you paved it so beautifully. To my assistant writer, dear friend and public relations cohort, Maria Evans, thank you for all your help on this project. To Michael Port and Priscilla Huff, thank you for serving as a mentors and for giving me so much inspiration.

To the book cover co-designers, Alexis "Lexie" Doyle and Pat Achilles, my favorite illustrator, it's exactly what I imagined. And to Kitty Mace, your guidance on layout and design has been invaluable.

To my colleagues and friends, Leah Rice, Brandyn Bissinger, Marisa Veni, Katherine Bellefontaine, Catherine Ponist, Donna Barnish, Toni Buckley, Roberta Perry, Dawn Byers, Kristen Egan, Katie Noonan, Chanin Walsh, Andy Cleff, Laura Powers, Megan Kristel, Krista Clark, Jim Turner, Joe Lanzalotti, Michael Pratt, Will Hornsby, Rich Klein, Mark Tarasiewicz, Dan Cirucci, Robin Nolan, Joe Stampone, Jeanne Bryan, Alan Rutkin, Rhonda Hill Wilson, Ross Fishman, Sayde Ladov, Kevin O'Keefe, Rudy Garcia, Chuck Polin, Alan Feldman, Jason Lisi, Susan Williams, Karen Friedman, Molly Peckman, Debbie Russo, Gayle Crist Shisler, and all of my colleagues in the Women's Business Forum of Bucks County who have encouraged me from the very start, thank you for all of your support.

One of my favorite quotes comes from the movie *Forrest Gump:* "Life is like a box of chocolates...you never know what you're gonna get!" I couldn't have scripted my life any better, and although I didn't know where the road would take me, I know I certainly love where I am. So, to my husband Scott, thank you for all of your infinite support, encouragement, sacrifice and belief in me. I thank God every day for you, our children and that box of Ghirardelli Chocolates.

To our children, Gianna and Ford, you are my purpose. You are our first loves. You are my magic, my dreams, my sunrise and my sunset. Follow your dreams and always remember to love who you are. I do.

To my mother, thank you for being such an integral part of our lives. You are my angel. Your beauty and sacrifice are endless. To my father, thank you for paving the way. I'm honored to follow in your footsteps. To Bernadette, my second mother, thank you for being there for us. You always make us smile. To Gretchen, Gayle, Dan, Walter and Louise, thank you for your infinite support.

And to the memory of each of my grandparents, Guido and Yolanda (Giordano) Piccionetti and Edward and Mollie (Scola) Furia. I remember.

Welcome to the world of public relations for lawyers—a world that until recently contained a lot of uncharted territory. But, as you already know, rainmaking in this field isn't what it used to be. Attorneys today rely on marketing and public relations to attract and retain clients. Those who don't, fail to do so at their own peril.

Attorneys who received their J.D.'s prior to 1978 will tell you that, for them, public relations and marketing were considered unethical. These lawyers dreaded self-promotion. Similarly, those who followed them, earning their degrees between 1978 and 1998, probably never talked about marketing or public relations as crucial aspects of their business management and development plans. But today, attorneys routinely educate themselves about the ethics of communicating with potential and existing clients. These savvy lawyers know that public relations, marketing and advertising are key components of developing new business and becoming rainmakers.

As a third-generation attorney, I've had the privilege of watching this fascinating evolution. I have seen public relations and marketing change from taboo topics to grudgingly accepted practices to tools that no lawyer can afford to ignore. My grandfather, Edward W. Furia, graduated from University of Pennsylvania Law School in 1930 and practiced law until 1971, when he became the first Italian-American U.S. Magistrate for the Eastern District of Pennsylvania. When he practiced, he simply hung a shingle outside of his Broad Street office in South Philadelphia. He listed his name in the telephone book white pages (and this only because he maintained an account with the Bell Atlantic telephone company). And he went to Palumbo's, the neighborhood social club, with my grandmother, Mollie, every Saturday night, where he frequently entertained legal questions from friends and acquaintances in the community. These same folks later arrived at his office and became clients of the firm. That was rainmaking.

In 1971, my father, Richard F. Furia, took over my grandfather's practice. Growing up the son of a lawyer, my father was raised with the view that all of his business would come from family, friends and word-of-mouth in the neighborhood. But even then, he knew that he had to be visible, present and accessible. He gave time to everyone in need and worked hard to maintain the business. Yet he, too, was taught that it was unethical to advertise one's legal services. But in 1977, the U.S. Supreme Court decided Bates v. State Bar of Arizona. In Bates, a dispute over a newspaper advertisement led a divided Court to rule that the First Amendment permits lawyers to advertise their services (with limitations).

Fast-forward to 1994, when I received my J.D. We still weren't taught anything about business management or communications in law school. As a matter of fact, in 2007, a large number of articles surfaced about business development teachings in law schools. When I was a student, we were taught about leaps and bounds, offer and acceptance, causation and damage, the Rule of Perpetuities and the art of advocacy in the courtroom. We graduated without even considering how to promote, sustain or grow our practices. Fortunately, I was a corporate communications major as an undergraduate student at Drexel University in Philadelphia, so I had a solid foundation in business communications. I knew that growing my legal practice would take focused effort and expertise that I had not gained in law school. Today I assist attorneys who similarly realize that the competitive local, national and international legal marketplaces require strategic planning to bring in and retain clients. Like you, these lawyers are ready to make public relations and marketing a prominent element of their business plans. So, let's get to work.

PART ONE
THE PLANNING AND PROCESS OF PUBLIC RELATIONS

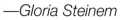

CHAPTER ONE

"Without leaps of imagination, or dreaming,
we lose the excitement of possibilities.
Dreaming, after all, is a form of planning."
—*Gloria Steinem*

Strategic Public Relations: A Primer

Before you sit down with this book and start dreaming about all the television, radio and print outlets in which your name and face are going to appear, take a step back and start thinking strategically. Really, when was the last time you walked into a jury trial without years (or at least months) of preparation? Much like a successful trial outcome, positive publicity can only be achieved through focused, sustained effort. It's important that your expectations are reasonable. In addition, you need to understand that the fruits of your public relations efforts need to grow before they will be ripe for picking, and the growing season depends upon the climate in which they're planted.

So let's begin at the beginning by explaining what is meant by public relations, or "PR," and how it differs from marketing and advertising.

Defining Public Relations

Public relations is the art and science of proactive advocacy on the part of a company, individual or brand. It requires strategic management of your position statement and key messages in order to reach your target audiences, and through various tactics, establish good will and a mutual understanding. In short, effective use of public relations tools allows us to shape public opinion, attitudes and beliefs. Utilizing public relations is much like crafting an opening statement for a jury trial: you will painstakingly strategize about which facts you should initially reveal to the jury, which heartstrings (if any) you want to tug, the tempo and timing of your delivery, and the information you deliver last in order to achieve a long-term impact.

In the big scheme of legal communications, "marketing" is the overall umbrella term under which many forms of communications fall. The "marketing" of a law firm often entails:

- Advertising
- Business Development
- Client Services
- Marketing (brochures, Web sites, direct mail, etc.)
- Sponsorships
- Public Relations

The public relations portion of your firm's marketing must be a strategic part of a carefully considered marketing plan so that it complements the branding, advertising, business development, client services, sponsorships and other communication initiatives. The role of public relations is to help build the firm's brand equity by delivering key messages to target audiences to elicit a particular response and thus shape public opinion, attitudes and beliefs. In other words, PR is the method by which we communicate messages about ourselves, our firms, and our understanding of the law and the cases we handle on an everyday basis. The practice of public relations differs from marketing and advertising. PR promotes and builds awareness and acceptance; the immediate goal is often based in the positioning of the firm; you have less control over the media placements; and the messages tend to be viewed as more credible.

MARKETING AND ADVERTISING VS. PUBLIC RELATIONS

MARKETING/ADVERTISING	PUBLIC RELATIONS
Promotes the transfer of legal services from the lawyer/law firm to the consumer	Promotes a firm/attorney to its public to build awareness and acceptance
Immediate goal is to generate new business	Immediate goal is mutual understanding or positioning of the firm/attorney with its publics
Implicit goal is profit	Implicit goal is positive perceptions and awareness to support the marketing goal of profit
Can control the message and the medium (advertising/direct mail)	Much less control over the message and the medium—with media relations, you're at the mercy of the media outlet (TV/radio/newspaper)
Measure of success is the amount of sales/revenue/funds it generates	Measure of success is expressed in public opinion, support, awareness, acceptance and media coverage

Your first step in harnessing the power of public relations will be to create a solid foundation on which to build. In this and other ways, creating a public relations plan is like building a new house. It is a very exciting time that requires financing, strategic thinking, careful planning and follow-through. It requires time, attention and measurable objectives.

Creating a Strong Foundation

When you decide you are going to build a house, you first have to determine how much money you will spend. This requires evaluating your income, expenses and future needs and allowing for the unexpected. Once you know your budget, you will need to determine where you want to live and whether that piece of land will support the house you wish to build. You will next have to engage the right contractors and engineers to test the soil, draw up the plans, get the necessary permits and so on.

You'll determine where your house should be located, the style of home you want to build, and the number and size of the rooms you will need to accommodate your long-term plans. You will next determine the type of foundation you will need. The specifics like framing materials, exterior parameters, plumbing and heating will need to be determined. You will do all this and more before you ever decide on the interior details such as color, trim, lighting, floors and window treatments. This is no different than strategic and measurable public relations planning.

So, as we explore this topic, you should keep two things in mind: first, an end result—such as being quoted in the press—is the same as color, trim, lighting, floors and window treatments. You don't get there without first going through the planning process. Second, like real property, public relations is an investment, not an expense.

Thinking Strategically: The Whys and Hows of Public Relations Strategy

Strategy can be defined as the determination of the basic long-term objectives of your firm's communications efforts. Who are your target audiences and what would you like them to do in response to your message? Strategy also includes the allocation of resources necessary to carry out your plan, a determination of a manageable timeline and the designation of the benchmarks you will set in order to measure the success of your efforts. Your strategy will be used to reach your target audiences and convey your messages, as well as to form the foundation of your public relations plan. You certainly would not begin to build the walls of your house without first identifying where the house should be located, the style of home you want to build, the number and size of the rooms you need, and the type of foundation you need to build a home that will stand for centuries.

The tools we use to deliver public relations strategies are called tactics. These tools are like the special amenities we use to enhance our homes. We might install crown molding, granite countertops and custom cabinets to add beauty and value to our homes. Similarly, we can use publicity, community relations, special events, speaking engagements, sponsorships and other forms of proactive advocacy to mold public opinion.

It should be noted, however, that reactive, ad-hoc public relations tactics—sending out a press release, staging an open house, sponsoring a continuing legal education program, hosting a press conference—are rarely effective and sometimes dangerous without having first determined your strategy. It's like purchasing furniture for your home before you have a floor plan.

Just as we cannot expect a house to be built in one day, we must also realize that public relations will not increase business overnight. Harnessing the impact and power of public relations is a long-term, strategic commitment that incorporates many different approaches to achieve a firm's goals. Thus, you build the sustainable house.

Public relations, when done right, will allow you to build a portfolio of news clippings and article reprints that helps to objectively establish credibility. Correctly employed and executed, public relations will raise awareness about your legal services and will position you as a leader in an ever-growing marketplace. Public relations is particularly beneficial for lawyers because it promotes legal services and their importance to the marketplace and the community at large. Be certain, however, to remain within the bounds of the restrictive codes of professional conduct.

Your strategy is the blueprint of your public relations home. The tactics are the amenities, furniture and decorations that allow you to reap the benefits. This book explores how you can employ different tactics to reach your target audiences as part of a strategic public relations plan. Right now, the focus is on the strategic planning process.

Planning for Public Relations

A solid public relations program should:

- Build awareness of your firm and your services

- Position you as knowledgeable within your areas of practice

- Position you as a valuable contributor to the legal profession

- Create an environment that will enhance good will among your target audiences

- Educate and persuade your target audiences

- Have a measurable value to you and your firm

So let's get started in determining the specs for your new public relations plan.

Strategic Public Relations, One Step at a Time

In order to develop and execute a strategic public relations campaign, you must employ an eight-step process. These steps are essential to developing a measurable and sustainable public relations plan.

1. Establish your goals and objectives.

2. Define how you want to be perceived.

3. Determine your target audiences.

4. Establish your key message—what do you want and need to say?

5. Decide what you want your target audiences to do.

6. Identify which tactics will persuade your target audiences to act in the desired manner.

7. Implement each tactic to generate optimal results.

8. Measure your successes against your goals and objectives.

Returning to the home-building analogy, first determine where you want to live (Strategy). Then decide what type of house you want to live in (Perception/ Position). Next, define who will live in the house (Target Audiences). Then explain to the architect how you want to live and how you plan to use your living space (Key Message). The architect will design your home and grounds so that you can use it the way you would like (Call to Action). The builder will build the house so that you will enjoy the space in the intended manner (Tactics). Once the house is complete, it will be furnished and decorated with the amenities that allow you to live in style and comfort (Implementation). Finally, when all is said and done, walk across the street, look up at the house and say, "Wow, what a great investment we've made in our new home! It has already appreciated in value and was a sound use of our resources." (Measurement)

What all this means is that your public relations plan needs to fit into your firm's business and marketing plans. The purpose of the plan is to state your goals and detail how they will be achieved. You must adopt a proactive mind-set, not a reactive one. Look for ways to get out in front of a story or opportunity. Create your own news and events. Set the agenda. Frame the issue.

And, as you communicate, it is crucial that you not go to press conferences, interviews or television appearances without first being media-trained. The same goes for your spokespeople.

THE FOUR P'S OF MEDIA TRAINING

Media training involves preparation, practice, planning and performance. Media training teaches how to conduct an interview; how to appear on television; how to communicate your message effectively and persuasively through verbal, vocal and visual skills; how to overcome physical and verbal roadblocks to effective communications; and more. It is very unprofessional to "wing it" and will likely work to your disadvantage. Consider how many times you have seen an attorney on the courthouse steps, covering the client's face with a briefcase while saying, "No comment." Not very effective, right?

Chapter 3 explores media training and the Four P's in detail.

To build your sustainable house, move on to the next chapter for a closer look at the eight steps.

CHAPTER TWO

" All things are possible until they are proved
impossible—and even the impossible
may only be so, as of now.
— *Pearl S. Buck* "

Building from the Ground Up: A Closer Look at the Eight Steps

Step 1: Establishing Your Goals and Objectives

Great public relations can substantially accelerate business development cycles, increase audience awareness and help promote rapid growth. Harnessing this power can be a terrific boost—if you proceed with clear objectives and remain true to your core business goals. You therefore need to ask yourself, "Will public relations help our firm achieve the goals we have set out in our business plan?" This is a good time to review or articulate your firm's core business goals. Understanding your business or performance goals is the first step in defining measurable objectives for a public relations program. When you measure the value of your public relations program, you need to substantiate that public relations has furthered your aspirations.

DEFINING YOUR BUSINESS GOALS

Q. What are your core business goals?

A. _____

_____

_____

_____

Now that you have identified your business goals, you need to determine your public relations objectives. What do you hope to accomplish by executing a public relations plan? What do you want people to think, say or do when they hear the name of your law firm (or visit your home)? Every attorney or managing partner should ask this question when embarking on a public relations program. The answers will help draft the blueprint of your plan and determine the best tools to implement it.

To get started, ask yourself how public relations programs can help achieve your core business goals. What can public relations do more effectively than other disciplines such as advertising? Once you've answered these questions, then you can move on to defining your public relations objectives. Typical public relations objectives for lawyers include:

- Increase awareness about your firm and services.

- Build name recognition of your firm and services.

- Communicate a merger, acquisition or office relocation to facilitate easy communication between your firm and its constituents.

- Increase new business and profits.

BUILDING FROM THE GROUND UP: A CLOSER LOOK AT THE EIGHT STEPS

- Retain existing clients.

- Acquire prospective clients in a new market segment.

- Develop employee goodwill.

- Garner media attention regarding a successful verdict
  to shape public opinion.

- Build a case where there are other possible plaintiffs such
  as class actions, Superfund matters and multiple-party matters.

- Generate referrals from other attorneys.

With the digital age of communication, public relations can also be used to create a two-way conversation with your target audiences.

DEFINING YOUR PUBLIC RELATIONS OBJECTIVES

Q. What do you want to achieve by conducting public relations?

A. _____

_____

_____

_____

So, now that you know what you want to achieve and why you want to achieve it, you need to decide how you want to be perceived: in other words, what style home do you wish to build?

Step 2: It's All About Perception

Do you have a contemporary or classical lifestyle? Do you want to live in farmhouse, new home or penthouse? Ask yourself what you want people to think, say or do when they hear about you, your firm or your services. How do you want to be positioned or perceived? What type of business lifestyle do you live? This is your position statement. For example, if your firm wants to be known for whistle-blower litigation, then you should craft your position statement around how you protect employees who report employer misconduct.

You also need to determine how you are currently perceived. Ask your significant other to tell you what you do. Jot down his or her response. Do the same thing with your best friend, closest neighbor, parents, employees, children and business associates. Get the picture? If everyone answers, "Well, you're a lawyer," then you are barely there. My response is, "So what?" It doesn't matter that you're "a lawyer." The question is: what purpose does your legal prowess serve?

If you are a general practitioner from the neighborhood or a high-powered corporate attorney who makes and generates multimillion-dollar deals, you need to be perceived as such. Or perhaps you would like to be known as the go-to attorney for local injured workers. At the end of the day, you want the most important audiences to perceive you the way you want and need to be perceived. In other words, if you can walk the walk, talk the talk for purchasers and potential purchasers of your services.

DEFINING HOW YOU WANT TO BE PERCEIVED

Q.   How do you want people to perceive you as an attorney?

A. _____

_____

_____

_____

Features vs. Benefits

Once you have decided how you want to be perceived, there are two things that you need to communicate in your position statement. These are the features of your firm and how they benefit your target audiences. Sales (a word that most attorneys loathe) teaches the promotion of the benefits and to back them up with the features. So then, what is the difference?

Although entire seminars and books are devoted to explaining the differences between features and benefits, here is the answer in a nutshell: features are the characteristics that physically describe your legal services, background or experiences.

For example, when you hold a crystal goblet in your hand, you know a feature is that it is crystal. Another feature is that it is clear. Yet a third feature is that it is solid. Just about every biography of an attorney describes the areas of law within which she practices, her education and professional background, the courts within which she is admitted to practice, a listing of any articles or treatises she has published, and the all-important number of years she has been in practice. Like it or not, most bios communicate features about the attorney—certainly not the benefits of working with her. The benefits of the crystal goblet are that you can see through the container to identify the liquid inside and that the goblet is weighted so that it cannot easily tip over.

Remember the house that you're building. The features are the number of rooms, the number of bathrooms, the size of the kitchen, the style of architecture, the fact that the home has air conditioning and gas heat, etc. The benefits are things like living in a preferred school district, having access to the public sewer instead of a septic system, the ability to expand, enjoying room to entertain, the fact that you have gas heat (which is less expensive than electric heat) and so on.

The benefits of working with you describe how your legal services will help your clients solve their problems. The benefits tell your audiences what they will gain by working with you or your law firm. Of course, the benefits language is more highly scrutinized in legal communications because you cannot present information that is subjective, creates an unjustified expectation, is false or misleading, compares your legal prowess to that of another attorney or firm, or omits necessary facts when the communication is considered "commercial speech." Just recently, I read a firm overview in which the firm described itself as "one of the region's most well-respected and rapidly growing" law firms. My initial reaction was, "Oh, really? Says who?"

In a nutshell, benefits tell the target audiences what you can do for them and why it matters. Benefits answer the "Who cares?" question. Features establish credibility and distinguish your background from that of your competitors. Just be careful that what you say complies with your state's professional rules and those of any additional jurisdictions in which you practice and communicate your services.

A final consideration when we talk about perception is whether your aspiration is reasonable.

I once had a plaintiffs' attorney from a relatively small town with a population of less than 9,000 people tell me that he wanted to be known as "the best" attorney in his state, which has a population of 12.3 million and nearly 50,000 licensed lawyers. He also thought he should be on CNN, MSNBC, "The Today Show" and "Good Morning America." Mind you, this attorney had also retired from the practice of law for several years and wanted to make "a comeback." Setting reasonable goals and objectives is half the battle in successful public relations planning. Don't try to build your house on a mountain known for mudslides.

Step 3: Friends, Family, Countrymen (and Women!): Defining Your Target Audiences

Who will live in your home and who will you invite to visit? With regard to your public relations efforts, do you know exactly who you want to influence? These people are better known as your target audiences, and they should be defined as precisely and accurately as possible. Your target audiences should be the thought leaders and decision makers who will ultimately affect your firm's bottom line. Other common names for such individuals are "influencers" and "stakeholders."

For most law firms, target audiences include current clients, prospective clients, referring counsel and firm employees. But what about the thought leaders who influence the decisions of your clients, prospects, referring counsel and employees? Don't forget about them. They can include clergy, union leaders, corporate executives, trade association leaders, community leaders, government officials, activists and the media, just to name a few.

DEFINING YOUR TARGET AUDIENCES

Q.   Who do you want to influence?

A.   _____

   _____

   _____

   _____

After you define each target audience, you need to dig a little deeper. This is the most difficult task for general-practice firms and larger firms because they usually consist of many practice areas, all with different audiences. When this is the case, it is important to break down each practice area and its corresponding target audiences.

To hit the mark with your public relations program, you should ask yourself the following questions about your target audiences:

- Where are my target audiences? Are they local, regional, national or even global?

- In which industries do my target audiences work?

- Are my target audiences made up of men, women or both?

- Where do my target audiences shop?

- What news publications and programs do my target audiences read, listen to and view?

- Which trade and consumer publications do my target audiences read?

- Do my target audiences subscribe to blogs, podcasts or other forms of electronic and social media?

- What conferences, seminars or town meetings do my target audiences attend?

- What are the age groups of my target audiences?

- Who influences the legal service buying decisions of my target audiences?

When you've answered all of these questions, then ask yourself one more:

- What are the needs of my target audiences and how can I meet them?

Step 4: Can You Hear Me Now? Establishing Your Key Messages

Once you have defined who you are trying to reach and how you want to be perceived, you will need to figure out what you want and need to say. This is traditionally referred to as establishing your "key messages."

Your key messages are thoughts, words or phrases that embody the main ideas that you and your firm would like to express to your target audiences. They must be clear, concise and memorable. Your key messages must also align with your business objectives. These are the thoughts that you want your audiences to remember above all else. They ensure consistency so that you and other members of your firm are speaking with one voice to your target audiences.

Your primary key messages will be part of the foundation of your public relations and marketing plans. Focusing on a few key messages is vital to effective communication. The primary key messages help hold up the house as it is being built. Through your primary key messages, you will communicate your overall message: who you are, what you do, what your clients need from you, and what services and benefits you will deliver to them.

BUILDING FROM THE GROUND UP: A CLOSER LOOK AT THE EIGHT STEPS

16

DEFINING YOUR KEY MESSAGES

Q. What do you want and need to say?

A. _____

_____

_____

_____

Building on your primary key messages, you should also create secondary key messages that communicate the nature of underlying or derivative needs. The secondary key messages are used to communicate specific needs or wants that may arise during the course of your business practices. They reinforce your primary key messages and then focus on a particular issue, fact or matter. For example, you might want in-house counsel for national banks to be aware that your firm served as outside counsel in a successful national bank merger. Your firm is still conveying the primary key message that you handle mergers and acquisitions; however, your secondary key message will be tailored to the particular event rather than the overall nature of your firm.

Your secondary key messages should vary depending on what you're trying to accomplish.

As a second example of a tailored message, consider a firm that handles general plaintiffs' matters. If the firm would like to begin picking up class-action cases, a secondary key message would be tailored to the potential class-action suit itself. Thus the message might focus on a Superfund site, a prescription drug or unfair trade practices.

Once you have determined the key messages that reinforce your goals and objectives and that are tailored to the needs and wants of your target audiences, you will need to determine what you want your audiences to do in response to your messages.

Step 5: The Call to Action: Determining What You Want Your Target Audiences to Do

Ask yourself what you want your target audiences to think, say or do when they hear your message. Do you want them to call your office to join a class-action lawsuit, or do you want them to refer a certain type of business to your firm? Or would you just like them to be aware that you exist, in case they need your services in the future?

Understanding what you want to happen as a result of communicating your key messages is no different than inviting people to your new home for dinner. You are asking them to come to your home at a certain time, on a certain date, to partake in a defined event.

DEFINING YOUR CALL TO ACTION

Q. What do you want your target audiences to think, say or do
    as a result of your message?

A. _____

    _____

    _____

    _____

So, now that you have identified what you want to accomplish; what you want to say; who you want to reach; and what you want them to think, say or do when they hear your message, you must determine how you will convince them to respond. In other words, which tactics will effectively reach them and how are you going to build the house?

Step 6: Tactical Maneuvers: Persuading Your Target Audiences to Act

There are many public relations tactics you can employ to create an ongoing buzz. Tactics designed to increase awareness among your target clients, generate recognition and position you as an authority in the industry will inevitably build your firm's book of business. By consistently and effectively executing strategic public relations tactics, you can build momentum and increase your bottom line.

The best way to determine which tactics will work for you is to identify the typical activities, desires and needs of your target audiences.

Earlier, we talked about how to determine who your target audiences are; now you need to determine what they want and need. You don't have to invest a lot of money to make this determination. Do some research. Ask your ideal clients what they respond to. Ask thought leaders in your sphere of influence what makes them tick. Conduct secondary research to uncover general data that will help you make the right decisions. Most importantly, determine and articulate what pains you can alleviate and what problems you can solve on behalf of your clients.

Also, find out if members of your target audiences tend to be avid viewers of local or national television news. Or are they Gen Y'ers who get their news from the World Wide Web? Do they religiously attend particular industry conferences, do they have a savvy public relations program for which they would publicize an award, or are they networking regularly within an industry association?

If you want to generate publicity that will reach your target audiences, ask yourself which publications they typically read. Much of this information is available in the press kits used to solicit advertising for print, television, radio and online outlets. If you're reaching out to referring counsel, are they reading The National Law Journal and Lawyer's Weekly USA or are they watching CNN and MSNBC news? Once you know which publications your target audiences read, which television programs they watch, and which radio broadcasts they listen to, you can target your media outreach to those outlets.

It is also important to identify who is making the decisions to hire legal counsel in their households or companies. You should recognize and understand the trends in your target audiences' lives and businesses and decide which types of programs (tactics) you can develop to respond to those trends.

EVERYDAY PUBLIC RELATIONS FOR LAWYERS

In order for you to be a part of the messages getting through to your target audiences, you need to execute the strategic tactics that will get their attention. Common public relations tactics include:

- Media Relations/Publicity
- Speaking Engagements
- Special and Community Events
- Awards Programs
- New Media/Digital Communications.

In order to understand which tactics are right for you, go back and ask, "What am I trying to accomplish?" When you are an associate, for example, you may have a very limited amount of time to devote to public relations efforts. So you may decide that one or two simple tactics like writing legal articles and having them published in a trade or consumer magazine is all you can really do. You may also be limited to personal networking, such as joining a book club, playing in a weekend basketball league, or staying in touch with friends and acquaintances from high school, college and law school. As your career matures, however, you will begin looking to your firm's culture and expectations to help define what you should be doing to enhance your name and stature in the community.

On the other hand, if you work in a firm that has a marketing department, now is the time for you to meet with the marketing director and ask what you can do to assist with regard to public relations. In larger firms, it is not the attorney's job to issue press releases or organize continuing-education programs to reach your target audiences. Your firm will have procedures in place (and, if not, it is time to establish them) for all of the marketing and public relations programming. The marketing director will likely be thrilled if you avail yourself.

In the larger firms, it is likely that the firm will dictate what type of public relations you should pursue, but you can find opportunities by analyzing who you are and where your interests lie. Ask yourself: "What are my passions? How can I parlay them into promotional opportunities? What industries are most appealing to me?"

BUILDING FROM THE GROUND UP: A CLOSER LOOK AT THE EIGHT STEPS

Most of the time, you will want to employ multiple tactics so you're not just a blip on your audiences' radar screen. You want more than just 15 minutes of fame.

Step 7: Working It: Using Tactics to Generate the Best Results

Implementation is the "how-to" in public relations. It is the actual execution of each tactic to reach your target audiences with your key messages in order to effectuate your goals and objectives. The majority of this book is dedicated to implementation—always keeping in mind the need for solid strategy first.

Step 8: The Payoff: Measuring Your Results against Your Goals and Objectives

With the pressure to be competitive and acquire and retain more and more clients, law firms know they must execute their marketing and public relations plans thoroughly. But few take the time to measure the effectiveness of their communications. How do you know for certain that 40 percent of new cases came from referrals or that the seminar you hosted did or did not generate new clients?

If you don't measure the effect of your public relations, you are only half-communicating. You created a solid public relations plan, targeted your audiences, identified your positions, crafted your messages, laid out your calls to action, and executed a long list of tactics. But that's only half the job. In order to complete the process, you must measure the results. Without measuring results, you are wasting the money you spent on creating and implementing your plan in the first place.

So, let's get on with the program. Let's make the investment to build your strategic, sustainable and influential public relations house.

CHAPTER THREE

> A masterpiece is something said once
> and for all, stated, finished, so that it's there
> complete in the mind, if only at the back.
> —*Virginia Woolf*

Putting the Media to Work for You

When the opportunity to work with the media arises, you need to be well prepared and media-trained to ensure that everything will run smoothly and effectively. I encourage every firm, no matter how big or small, to have a written media policy. Simply put, law firms and their attorneys can and should control all messages provided to the media for reasons of message management, ethics and, in the cases of trial publicity, to protect the clients' best interests.

A Media Policy Primer

Your firm's media policy should address:

- Who may speak with the media on the firm's behalf
- The procedures that members of your firm must follow when the media calls
- Record-keeping procedures for media calls and interviews

- How you handle calls about specific firm clients and/or cases
- How you handle calls for third-party commentary on specific cases or legal issues
- Crisis communications procedures
- The ethics of dealing with the media

Public relations is a productive way to enhance an individual's or firm's professional reputation. If you are interested in increasing your media exposure, this is most easily accomplished by developing personal relationships with members of the media.

Creating a Media List

With a media relations campaign, you don't control the final message the way you do with a paid advertisement. When you advertise, you decide when, where, what and how your message will appear. But when a media outlet runs a story about you or your legal matter, you get the benefit of an apparently objective third-party endorsement. The public tends to give greater weight to media-provided information than to advertisements.

In order to maximize the value of your media relationships, take heed of the following tips.

Determine your primary geographic market: This could be a particular city, a geographic region or a national audience.

Create your general media list: Put together a list of newspapers, television and radio stations, newsletters, magazines, blogs and e-zines that reach your target markets. There are publications and databasesavailable that include listings of media contacts such as MediaAtlas (mediatlas.prnewswire.com), Cision (formerly Bacon's, www.cision.com) and others.

Double-check your contact file: Verify your list of contact names, addresses and phone numbers, and make sure they cover your topic or industry.

Know who you're pitching: Become familiar with the media outlets on your list. Read the publications and blogs, watch the television programs, listen to the radio shows and get to know their individual content and style, especially that of the reporters you plan to pitch.

Update your list regularly: Update your list at least quarterly and anytime you make media calls and find out that someone new is covering your industry. Job changes are common in journalism, especially in light of the continuing decline in print advertising sales, which has led to frequent restructuring and consolidation of media outlets and their publishers.

Once you've assembled your media list, double-checked it, and gotten to know who you're pitching and why, you can use it to send out news about your business, story ideas and trends to the media outlets that cover your issues.

Reaching Out to the Media

"Good press" is a vital component of legal communications, and in order to obtain it, you must understand how to best relate to reporters. "Pitching" a reporter or producer in public relations is akin to throwing a ball to the batter to see if she's going to hit it and, if so, how far. Even though the commonly known terminology is "pitching," think of it more as the art of communicating and having a conversation. There is no single way to pitch the media. Understanding some of the nuances of the media will help you become a better communicator in the long run.

Understand deadlines: The worst time to contact a reporter is when she is "on deadline." If you try to contact a reporter who's on deadline, most likely she will not be very receptive to your story. Always ask whether it is a good time before discussing your story with a reporter. If the reporter says it's a bad time, ask when a better time would be for you to call back. Be sure to call back at that time.

Be memorable: Reporters receive hundreds of calls, phone calls, e-mails and faxes every week, so it is important that your story stands out from the rest. Research the reporter before contacting her. Know the reporter's beat (in other words, what types of articles she writes and where she obtains her information). Be familiar with articles that the reporter has written in the past and, if you can, tie one of them in with your pitch. Be specific and brief—this will show the reporter that you are not wasting her time.

Know media frequency: It is also helpful to understand that a reporter working for a daily publication or newscast will be very interested in a news story that she can break to the public. On the other hand, reporters working for weekly publications or feature programs are more interested in detailed, comprehensive information and how that information will affect the business community. Be sure to modify your story and strategy accordingly.

Don't sell anything: When you're providing the media with news or a resource for information, you're not selling your firm's services. Don't send brochures, newsletters, practice descriptions or other marketing materials. Engage them in meaningful conversation that will help them tell your story or make you a go-to resource to be quoted in other stories.

Using Voicemail to Pitch Effectively

Understanding the general nature of media pitching is important. You should also understand that even your voicemail pitch must follow certain guidelines to be effective. Here are some principles to live by.

Be brief: Get to your point very quickly. Lead with your strengths. Don't try to tell the whole story in the message; just say enough so the reporter will call you back. On voicemail, the less said, the better.

Be memorable: The tone, volume and pitch of your voice are just as important as your message. Sound enthusiastic. Sound like you care about the story. Then, say one thing that will be memorable to the listener—speak in sound bites.

Make it easy: Make it easy for the reporter or producer to call you back quickly. Always leave your phone number twice and state the numbers clearly and slowly. It's very frustrating to have to replay the message. If you're working on a breaking news story, leave your home and cell numbers, too. It's okay to say, "I can be reached until 9 p.m. and after 7 a.m. tomorrow" to set parameters for times to be called back.

Call again: Don't leave a second voicemail unless it is absolutely necessary because you have new information to share. Rather, call again until you actually speak to the person—only when calling an office phone. If the reporter works from home or via a personal cell phone, try to reach him or her via e-mail before you call again. If you don't have any luck, put a day between your calls. This is media pitching, not stalking. When all else fails, you can try sending your pitch via overnight delivery service—which is rarely used and really gets attention.

Using E-mail to Pitch Effectively

Have you ever taken a vacation and come back to hundreds of e-mails in your inbox? For many journalists, producers and other media professionals, regardless of the medium, that's what their inboxes look like on an average day. So why do you think your e-mail is going to stand out above the rest? Again, there are some general rules you can follow, but pitching by e-mail is just as chancy as leaving a voicemail. It may or may not get through the SPAM filters at the other end, and when it does, it may or may not be read. Here are some ways to keep you out of the SPAM filters and junk box and to get you into the minds of the journalists.

Personalize, personalize, personalize: When you send an e-mail to a journalist, start with "Dear [insert name of reporter here]," and include a paragraph that introduces the most important aspect of your story and why it should matter to that journalist and her readers, viewers or listeners. At the close of your message, be sure to include ALL of your contact information.

One is enough: Never send your e-mail to more than one person at a time. It's obnoxious to see 50 e-mail addresses in the "To" field. It is frowned upon to "Bcc" your entire list of contacts with no personal message in the body copy. Pitch only one person at a particular media outlet. They all work together. If the story is not right for one, she will usually pass it on to someone else if it's right for the medium.

Keep it short: Keep your e-mail as short as possible. If you need to include a press release or other detailed information, include it in the body of the e-mail. Do not attach anything—especially if you are reaching out to the reporter for the first time. Many SPAM filters are now programmed to eliminate attachments, including PDFs. You can include a link to information on your firm's Web site, but even then, SPAM filters may not let you through.

The subject is EVERYTHING: The subject line is the first thing that's read. If it says, "Firm press release" and that's it, the journalist's mental response will likely be, "oh, great, another one." Instead, use the catchy title of the release that you will have written after reading Chapter 8 of this book.

Understand deadlines: Just like calling a reporter, sending an e-mail pitch on deadline is the worst time to contact a reporter. You're just adding to the clutter *(see Common Industry Deadlines, page 29).*

Don't make reporters work harder than necessary—it only raises red flags: Always be up front. Don't make a reporter dig for information.

Know where the line is and take pains not to cross it: Make sure everything you send to the media is truthful. If someone asks you to do something that you are unsure about, check with the Public Relations Society of America (www.prsa.org), which offers ethical guidelines.

Use of these suggestions can help create a more positive response from reporters when pitching your story.

┃PUTTING THE MEDIA TO WORK FOR YOU

Common industry deadlines include:

- For daily newspapers, 3 p.m. should be avoided.

- For weekly magazines and newspapers, find out what day of the week they put the publication to bed.

- For monthly publications, call the receptionist and find out what week their deadline falls on.

- For television and radio, the time and frequency of the show determines when the producers are in the office. For example, some morning show producers start their day at 2 a.m. and end it at 10 a.m.

Seek Media Training: Know the Four P's

Media training involves preparation, practice, planning and performance. Each of these "Four P's" is an extremely essential component of effective media training. Media training teaches you how to conduct an interview, how to appear on television, how to communicate your message effectively and persuasively, how to overcome physical and verbal roadblocks to effective communications, and more. It is very unprofessional to "wing it" and will likely work to your disadvantage.

THE FIRST P: PREPARATION

In today's legal arena, it is necessary for lawyers who plan to speak with reporters to be media-trained. Less-than-ideal interactions with reporters will appear in stories and quickly spread to many recipients via the Internet. Articles containing poorly worded statements, incomplete thoughts or factually incorrect commentary can be and often are repeatedly re-published through e-mail, blogs, Web sites and the like. On the other hand, if you know how to effectively communicate with the media, you can generate a great deal of publicity for yourself and your law firm.

Know your key messages: Formulate three key messages prior to speaking with the media. Determine the most important points that you want to convey and write them down. This will help you prepare your thoughts and lead to a successful interview.

Research the reporter: Before an interview, research the reporter with whom you will be speaking so that you know what kind of stories she writes (hard-hitting or more conservative, for example). This will help you anticipate her questions and in turn will enable you to prepare your answers.

Anticipate key questions and prepare key answers: When you anticipate the questions that you will be asked, you can plan your answers so that they clearly and concisely convey your key messages. Practicing how you will answer questions (not memorizing them) will make the interview more efficient. Think before you speak.

THE SECOND P: PRACTICE

Use your questions and answers to practice mock interviews with your colleagues. Pretend you're preparing to be the witness in a cross-examination and have a colleague ask you all the questions you've come up with. Also ask your colleague to surprise with you with questions you may not expect. Then, draft answers to the five questions you dread the most and the five questions you would most like to answer. If your matter is controversial, be prepared to answer the ones you dread. If you are going to be interviewed for television, tape your mock interview the same way you would in a mock trial. Play it back and critique yourself. Then ask others to do the same.

THE THIRD P: PLANNING

Know when, where and how long your interview will be. If it's a telephone interview, be sure that you will be somewhere quiet where you have privacy and can stand while you speak. If it's a radio or television interview, arrive at least a half-hour prior to the scheduled time.

If you are being interviewed in your office, make sure it's in order and that all sensitive materials and files have been stored. Remember, you never get a second chance to make a first impression.

THE FINAL P: PERFORMANCE

When interviewed, speak clearly and slowly in a conversational tone. Once you have made your point, do not be intimidated by silence. Silence is not a bad thing during an interview. Silence is a tactic used by reporters to get you to talk, in the hopes of getting you to say something that you shouldn't have. This is no different than the same tactic attorneys use to intimidate witnesses during depositions and trial. Silence might also indicate that a reporter is formulating her next question or transcribing what you have just said. Regardless of the reason for it, do not feel that you must fill silence. Wait for the reporter to proceed.

Performance Tips to Control Your Message

Here are some additional performance tips that will help you control your message:

Be concise: When speaking to the media, be concise but do not leave out any vital information. You do not want a journalist to find out information on her own and then confront you with it when you are not prepared to answer questions.

Don't panic: Do not panic if you are asked a question during an interview that you do not know the answer to. Be honest and tell the reporter that you do not know the answer but that you would be happy to look into it and get back to her. Do not attempt to make up an answer. Never wing it.

Never say "no comment": An attorney should never say "no comment." When a lawyer says this, it is perceived as an attempt to hide something or avoid telling the truth. If something is confidential, then tell the interviewer that you cannot provide confidential information. Just don't say, "No comment."

Nothing is "off the record": There is no such thing as "off the record" when speaking with members of the media. If you say it, then there's always a chance that it will end up in print or be broadcast. If you don't want it repeated, just don't say it.

EFFECTIVE ALTERNATIVES TO "NO COMMENT"

- "I think it would be clearer if I first explained..."
- "I don't have all the facts to answer that question, but I can say..."
- "Actually, that relates to a more important concern..."
- "I wouldn't use that choice of words. If you are asking (rephrase), I can tell you that..."

Record it: If you're being interviewed in person, make sure to pull your trusty recorder out in plain sight of the reporter. In the event of a misquotation or factual mistake, you can easily supply the reporter with the recording and request a correction. If the reporter refuses, by all means go to the editor in charge. In addition, review your interview to make sure you haven't left out any vital information. Listen to your interview technique with a fresh ear. To record your telephone interviews, you can use a simple device from Radio Shack or go big league with Call Recording Director, but remember to check your state's rules for the legality of recording conversations, especially if you haven't engaged in full disclosure.

Use the reporter's name: When you speak with a journalist, use her first name and try to relate to her. The more you get to know reporters and become a resource to them, and the more they get to know you, the more likely they are to give you good coverage.

Understanding Media Terminology

There are quite a few terms that you should be familiar with before speaking to the media. Then, once you are familiar with these terms, it is important to have a conversation with the reporter to determine her meaning of the terminology.

For example, people often use the phrase "off the record," but what does this really mean to the reporter? That is what matters most.

On the record: "On the record" or "for the record" means that what you say is fair game and may be included in the story. Therefore, your comments should be accurate, concise and memorable. They are statements that you want the media to repeat.

Off the record: "Off the record" comments should be avoided at all costs. My personal preference is that attorneys never make "off the record" comments because they can always come back to bite you. If you don't want it out there, then don't put it out there. That's the bottom line!

Embargo: An "embargo" usually entails providing an advance copy of an important press release or other information to the media with the understanding that they will not release the story to the public until a specified date and time. When done right, you maintain control of when the story breaks, and you give the media enough time to conduct research, gather quotes and cover the story. On the other hand, you always risk a leak because there are no guarantees. A hungry member of the media could break embargo without repercussion.

Exclusive: An "exclusive" is when you give a particular media outlet the opportunity to be the first to break a story. It is the only outlet to get the interview. In fact, many journalists insist on exclusives. For example, you may need to determine whether you will give "The Today Show" vs. "Good Morning America" an exclusive.

Second-day story: A "second-day story" should turn hard news into a multifaceted story that blends the issues with human interest. It is an update with new information on a story that was previously told. A second-day story fills in gaps in the original story, provides another angle and shares expert opinion, data or other new information.

For attribution: "For attribution" is very similar to speaking "on the record." Essentially, the information provided by the source is to be quoted and attributed to the person making the statement. The statement is usually followed by, "You can quote me on that."

Not for attribution: The exact opposite of "for attribution" is "not for attribution." It is when you provide the media with information that can be quoted and/or used, but that same information cannot be attributed to the source. In this case, the information or statement should be preceded by, "You cannot quote me on this." Again, "not for attribution" can be a sticky way to present information to the media. If you don't want it attributed to you, then it's better left unsaid. If you do not wish to provide certain information, you might consider earning some brownie points with the reporter by suggesting an alternative source for her to consult.

On background: According to a colleague who is an undercover investigative reporter, "on background" means that she is not going to identify the source but is going to use all the information provided by the source. That is one reporter's view, of course. "On background" can also mean that the information will not be attributed or used. It really depends on the source's preference, and this should be clarified between the source and the reporter.

On deep background: For the most part, when you say you are providing information to a reporter "on deep background," it generally means that the information is not for the public, but it can be used by the reporter to enhance the story or get additional information from other sources. This is another example of a situation where, if you don't want it published, then it's better not to put it out there in the first place.

The general rule of thumb should be to believe that everything is on the record, fair game, quotable, available from someone else, attributable, and about the story, not you!

PUTTING THE MEDIA TO WORK FOR YOU

The Do's and Don'ts of Media Relations

Now that we've covered media lingo and some rules of thumb, let's talk about some additional do's and don'ts of media relations. Just like you, reporters have pet peeves. And just like the legal community, the media have their own norms and unwritten rules. The following do's and don'ts will help keep you out of trouble and garner goodwill among the journalists you work with during your career.

When communicating with the media, DO:
- Be truthful and likeable
- Avoid jargon
- Clarify misinformation
- Speak clearly
- Be responsive
- Use examples
- Use inflection, pitch and tone
- Use verbal pace and pause
- Sit or stand comfortably
- Be calm and polite
- Be passionate and energetic
- Focus on your agenda
- Be clear and concise

On the other hand, DON'T:
- Get rattled
- Say "no comment"
- Speak "off the record"
- Speculate or provide advice
- Fill dead air—silence is an option
- Play with your hair or an object in your hand
- Make distracting motions
- Use negative statements
- Sound smug or arrogant
- Say "um," "uh," "okay," "like," "you know," or "er"
- Nod your head during a question

EVERYDAY PUBLIC RELATIONS FOR LAWYERS

The Specifics of Television, Radio and Print

TELEVISION

If you are going to be interviewed on television, there are several additional guidelines you should follow:

Watch the show several times before you are scheduled to appear: It is important to know the key players and the format of the show.

Choose your messages with care: Television reaches a very general consumer viewer, and morning news tends to have a higher female demographic. The producers have chosen to interview you and your topic based on a topic that you have already agreed upon. You must stick to that topic only, or the reporter will cut you off and move on to a different segment.

Stay calm, cool and collected: Remember to stay still. Don't sway back and forth or shake your feet. Take deep breaths. Pause between thoughts. Address the interviewer. Never look at the camera or monitors unless instructed otherwise. Keep your body language open and relaxed. Smile if the subject matter calls for a smile.

Speak in short sound bites: Practice your topic in sound bites. Television is a great medium for short, quick sound bites that the viewers can remember. Television reporters are also looking for short, to-the-point sound bites. You'll rarely see a person talking for more than 9 to 10 seconds during a TV story. A good example of sound bites is included in Chapter 8 under the topic of press conferences.

Spare the details: Most television stories run for less than 90 seconds. TV reporters aren't looking for hours of drawn-out details. Be concise and get to your point.

Count 2 seconds before answering: The slight pause before you answer will make your responses sound fresh and thoughtful.

Use flags and bridges: Signal that a key point is coming up by flagging it with a phrase like, "the key point is," or link each answer to a positive message by using bridging phrases like, "but let me put this in perspective" or, "but the real problem is…".

SAMPLE FLAGS AND BRIDGES

- "Let's look at it from a broader perspective…"
- "The real problem is…"
- "Let's not lose sight of the underlying problem…"
- "There is another issue playing into this…"
- "The most important thing to remember is…"
- "I disagree. Just the opposite is true…"
- "I don't know about that… But what I do know is…"

Speak in plain English: The general television viewer speaks and reads at a 6th-grade level. Speaking in plain English will ensure that your message gets across. In other words, avoid legal jargon. It's important when dealing with print, TV or radio to speak in layman's terms so your audience understands you and so that your messages are clear *(see Legalese-Buster Plain English Glossary, page 38).*

Remember to highlight your firm name: When you are first introduced, the reporter will generally mention your name and the firm you come from. It is important for you to mention your firm's name when it is appropriate and comes naturally, so the viewing audience will remember it.

Focus on your objective: Don't get bogged down in statistics or lengthy explanations. Speak briefly, directly and to the point. Correct any misstatements or misperceptions. You should have prepared key messages before speaking to the media. Make sure you know what they are and that you get them across in your interview.

Here are some synonyms that will help you avoid using legalese in your communications:

Acquitted	Found not guilty
Affidavit	Signed statement under oath
Asserted	Said
Complaint	Allegations
Convicted	Found guilty
Damages	Losses
Data	Information or Facts
Defendant	Perpetrator
Deposition	Statement under oath
Discovery	Research
Judgment	Decision
Jurisdiction	The court with the authority
Plaintiff	Victim
Postponement	Delay
Precedent	Controlling decision
Predicament	Situation
Statute of Limitations	Deadline
Tort	Wrongdoing or Negligence

Beware of interviewing traps: Use your own words. Never repeat negative language or allow the reporter to put words into your mouth. Never lose your cool. Remember that nothing is ever off the record.

Plan your attire: Proper planning provides for a polished product.

Don't wear white: It glows and becomes the most noticeable thing on the television screen.

Don't wear black: It's too harsh and can absorb too much light. Other solid colors work best.

Don't wear busy patterns: Thin stripes, busy tweeds, and prints produce distracting on-screen effects. This applies to ties and prints on shirts. Pastel shirts work well on TV.

Don't wear bright reds: They "bleed" on camera and are distracting.

Wear makeup: If you don't wear powder on your nose, forehead and face, you will look shiny, oily and plastic. Make sure the powder makeup you use is the same color as your skin, not lighter or darker.

Keep your suit jacket buttoned: In general, your suit will look more symmetrical, and you will appear more professional and polished. And for men, this will keep your tie in place.

Watch other people being interviewed: Watch others on TV with the sound turned off to see which mannerisms are distracting to you. Then, avoid using any of the same distracting body language, facial expressions or movements during an interview.

Eat well and avoid coffee or milk: Don't do the interview on an empty stomach. Your growling stomach will distract you. Coffee can make you jittery or nervous; milk can make your mouth feel gummy and will make it harder to talk.

RADIO PROGRAMS

Like television, radio has its own norms and idiosyncrasies. Close your eyes and listen to a radio news broadcast. Listen to interviews. You want to be able to paint a visual picture with words and still keep your message simple and to the point. Keep the following guidelines in mind when seeking radio publicity.

Do your homework: Before you send out a press release or call local radio stations with a story, listen to their programs. Familiarize yourself with the station's reporters. Get to know the demographics of their listeners and informational needs. This will allow you to target those radio stations whose listeners are most likely to be interested in your message or story.

Make yourself known as a spokesperson for an issue or an area of law: Because of the immediacy of radio, news employees have precious little time to hunt down sources when a story breaks. If you readily come to mind, they are more likely to call you.

Understand what radio news is: Understand that your firm's story or event will not be discussed on the radio unless it has true news value. If there is a human-interest angle, find out who should be contacted and whether the station covers human-interest stories.

Don't send photographs: Sending photographs to radio stations is a waste of time and money. They will only be thrown out.

Be a good guest: Know your material and answer the host's questions with the listeners in mind. Keep your answers brief. Provide enough information so the listeners will have learned something. Thank the host for having you as a guest, and be sure to send a thank-you note after the interview.

Ask for a copy: Many radio stations will provide you with a digital copy of the program. Request information about the outlet's copyrights and whether or not you are permitted to utilize the materials for your own promotional purposes. You may be able to use the audio recording on your Web site. But before you do, make sure it would be of interest to your target audiences.

PRINT PUBLICATIONS

Print media can usually donate more space to a story than electronic counterparts. You can provide more information, photographs or other visuals to promote your story. The more interesting, the more likely the publication will cover your story. Keep the following tips in mind when dealing specifically with print media:

Go the extra mile—help reporters see both sides of the story:
Reporters must not mislead their readers. Therefore, think like a
journalist. You can help the reporter create a balanced story by
going the extra step and providing her with opposing perspectives.
Showing both sides of a story makes it hard for the reporter to
accuse you of being disingenuous or biased.

Don't ask to proof the story before it is published: Reporters
pride themselves on being accurate and professional and may find
it offensive to have their work proofed. Additionally, permitting a
source to proof a story is highly taboo, and many editors have said
they would fire a reporter for doing so. Fear not, however, as many
reporters will call to double-check names and facts before a piece
is published.

If you do your homework and keep the preceding guidelines in mind, you will
increase your chances of receiving the media attention you desire. Remember
to utilize as many media forms (radio, television, print, electronic) as possible.
The more your target audiences hear and see your name, the more new business
your efforts will generate.

CHAPTER FOUR

If you be pungent, be brief; for it is with words as with sunbeams—the more they are condensed, the deeper they burn.
—*Robert Southey*

Putting Your Pen to Paper

Writing often feels like a very daunting task to the busy attorney. When attorneys are told they should write an article on a particular topic, the reaction is often as if the attorney has been asked to eat nails. On the other hand, I have had the experience of working with attorneys who love to write more than they love to litigate. Think about it this way: if you have something to say and you want to say it to a particular audience as an authority on the matter, then putting your pen to paper is a very effective tool for getting your point across.

Since attorneys have learned the art of writing briefs (which aren't brief at all), the art of pleading everything under the sun, and the art of providing backup for our backup, written copy tends to be quite long and verbose. Breadth and depth is very important for legal pleadings and other forms of legal documents; however, just the opposite is required when writing for publication. The art of clear and concise copy will improve the overall comprehension and appearance of your written materials and will undoubtedly boost exposure, message recall and the overall efficiency of your public relations endeavors.

Here are some quick tips for crafting copy that is clear and concise:

- Define legal and technical jargon in easy-to-understand language. Google can help by getting you a list of definitions for your term on the Web. Simply type "define term" into a search. Add a practical example or image to your definition, and you can easily paint a picture in your readers' mind.

- Your readers would rather read a short, to-the-point piece than a long, drawn-out piece. One good way to reduce the length of your copy is to focus each piece on a single message point. In addition to your main story, you might repackage your piece into sidebars, lists, related stories, freestanding vignettes, fun facts or trivia.

- Paragraph length is among the most important signals you send to readers about how easy and interesting your copy will be to read. If your paragraphs are too thick, the information looks slow and uninviting. If they're all the same length, the information can feel boring. Vary their length to create a sound rhythm for your piece. A good rule of thumb is that shorter is better. Try to keep your paragraphs to three sentences or so, and keep in mind that one-sentence paragraphs are usually perfectly acceptable.

Here are some forms of public relations writing that you can use to generate a buzz about you and your business.

The Authoritative Article

Writing authoritative articles is one of the easiest and most effective ways to garner valuable publicity—especially if you like to write. When an article is published and you haven't paid for the space (as opposed to placing an advertisement), you immediately establish credibility with your target audiences. It positions you as an expert without you saying, "Hey, look at me, I'm an expert on this topic." When you read Chapter 11 on ethics, you will see that calling an attorney an expert can get you into hot water.

The FAQ Response Method

The most common dilemma that attorneys face is what to write about. There are many ways to come up with topics for your articles, but my favorite puts strategy into play. I call it "the FAQ Response Method." I tell clients to keep a notebook next to the telephone they use the most at work. Keep the pages divided by topics such as client management, legal issues, practice areas, etc. Create two columns. In the first column, write down every question you are asked by a prospective or current client. In the second column, record the number of times you're asked the same question.

Once you've heard the question at least three times, draft your answer or record yourself answering the question into your Dictaphone and have it transcribed. Refine your answer and then research which publications, blogs, E-zines or Web sites deal with similar topics that reach your target audiences.

When writing for a print publication, be sure to read and review several previous editions in order to get a feel for the types of articles that are typically included.

Research the editorial guidelines (a.k.a. writers' guidelines) for your target publications, which are usually on their Web sites, and then follow those guidelines to refine your article. These are the rules that publishers provide to contributing authors *(see Editorial Guidelines, page 46)*.

It is important to comply with the editorial guidelines of your target publication in order to maximize your chances of publication. If you're not sure about something, contact the editor and ask. It's a great way to open the door to conversation and to offer yourself as available for commentary on similar issues while getting the editorial information you need to submit your article. You should also remember not to boast or overtly promote your firm or your services. Such behavior, whether in writing an article or when speaking at a seminar, is not appropriate.

EDITORIAL GUIDELINES

Some of the common matters addressed by editorial guidelines include:

- Length of article: the minimum and maximum word count. An optimum number of words per article might also be listed

- Editorial calendars, which include topics, themes, article types and required submission dates broken down by publication date

- Preferred format of articles for submission

- Topics accepted by the publication

- Copyright rules

- Use of illustrations and photographs

- Editorial style, such as compliance with "The Associated Press Stylebook and Libel Manual" for abbreviations, capitalization, grammar, punctuation and spelling

- Inclusion of an author's biography and head shot

- Compensation

- Query and submission requirements

So, if you represent corporations and work with in-house counsel, perhaps some of the questions (FAQs) you are used to hearing are:

- Does your firm offer alternative billing strategies?

- How does your firm protect the interests of your clients above and beyond the matters you're currently dealing with?

- How can we protect our company in light of Sarbanes-Oxley (SOX)?

This list goes on and on. A savvy attorney will then take the questions and turn them into answers that can be utilized by the masses within the industry. For example:

- What Clients Need to Know about Alternative Billing Strategies

- Protecting Clients' Interests above and beyond Traditional Representation

- Getting and Staying on Board with SOX

The TOC Review Method

Another way to determine what topic to write about is to review the table of contents (TOC) of the last six issues of a publication that your audiences reads—whether it's the local Sunday newspaper or a monthly trade magazine. I call this "the TOC Review Method." Then, answer the following questions:

- Are there any trends in these publications?

- What is the marketplace thinking about?

- How are themes being positioned locally, regionally, nationally?

- How can I expound on some of these issues?

- What can I say that is different, sheds light on the issue, informs the audiences and positions me as a go-to person in the field?

The Personal Experience Method

All articles are either written based on one's firsthand knowledge or a great deal of research. Another method that I like for determining what to write about is "the Personal Experience Method." This provides anecdotes, advice or ideas based on your experiences using actual examples (i.e., your personal experience). This is a great way to educate your target audiences and to share your legal prowess. This method can also be used to highlight your successes, with the permission of your clients, in the form of case studies.

A way to determine which personal experiences matter is to think about what you do as a part of your practice that is worth sharing with others. It's the "who cares" factor. If someone will care and can benefit from your knowledge and experience, then it's probably worth sharing.

Here are some questions to get you started:

- Have you successfully adjudicated a nonconfidential case with a complex set of circumstances? How? Why does it matter?

- Have you successfully picked a jury in a jurisdiction known to have certain biases? What were your tactics?

- Have you created a process or procedure to choose qualified vocational experts? What do you look for?

- Have you mastered a formula for any stage of the litigation process that is nontraditional?

So, now that you know how to come up with your topics, perhaps it is time for you to get to work.

Getting published is a rewarding way to gain positive publicity. I can still remember when my first public relations article was published by *Lawyers Weekly USA*. I was unbelievably happy and received tons of great feedback. I received calls from prospective clients, e-mails from current clients, and accolades from colleagues and friends. The article eventually led to new business, which more than established a solid return on investment for the time spent writing and placing the article—not to mention the purchase of reprints.

The Opinion Editorial
An op-ed (opinion-editorial) is a form of writing that is used to express a personal opinion. It is an underutilized and extremely powerful way to publish an attorney's opinion and demonstrate her depth of knowledge on a particular topic. In this way, the attorney is positioned as a thought leader in her area of expertise.

PUTTING YOUR PEN TO PAPER

An op-ed is located in the opinion pages of a newspaper, which is one of the most widely read sections. The op-ed submissions that get published deal with often-controversial topics of current interest and take a stand on the issues addressed. It is your opinion, so make it stick. Also keep in mind that you need to be quite careful if your op-ed deals with a topic that you are currently litigating. Do not write op-eds that pertain to any current client matters.

Since newspapers get countless op-ed submissions, getting one published can sometimes be difficult. When writing an op-ed, you should follow some basic guidelines to increase the odds that it will get published.

Be opinionated: The more rare or controversial your opinion, the more likely the op-ed will be published.

Write about one thing: If you cannot sum up your ideas in the headline, then it's probably not the best topic to choose for an op-ed.

Write in the active voice: It is easier to read.

Make a point that is unique: Prior to submitting your column, research what the publication has recently published on your topic. You do not want to repeat what others have already said about the same subject.

Keep it around 700 words: Typically an op-ed column should consist of about 700 words, although they can run longer, depending on the outlet. Keep in mind that newspapers have limited space to offer, and most of the time, editors will not take the time to cut an article down to size. You can determine the exact parameters by obtaining the submission guidelines, which are available in each publication and often on their Web sites.

Stay focused: Your op-ed needs to stay focused. Don't derail the train by trying to provide too much backup or writing as if you are presenting an opening statement. It's the short, concise closing arguments that are the most memorable after all.

Be timely: If you are writing about an event in today's news, then you must submit your editorial in a timely fashion—either the same day or a couple of days later. Op-eds deal with what's happening today, so don't get stuck commenting on yesterday's news.

Connect locally: Use the local approach when writing for a newspaper within your circulation area. Tie your commentary to local events and make sure you include your place of residence and why the issue matters to you. Many lobbyists and special interest groups write op-eds as part of their regular outreach strategy. Local papers are more likely to publish a column by a local author than by a lobbyist.

Here are some additional tips to follow when submitting your op-ed:

Know your audience: It is important to choose the right publication for your op-ed. Submit your piece to only one outlet. Ask yourself who's reading the publication and why you want them to read what you have to say. What are you trying to accomplish? If you're a local plaintiffs' firm, stick to the local newspapers. More people in your target demographic will read them than *The New York Times* or *The Wall Street Journal*. However, if you serve as national defense counsel for insurance providers, you may be better served with an article in a trade publication such as *ROUGH Notes* or a national newspaper such as *The Wall Street Journal* or *The New York Times*.

Define who cares: Explain why the publication's readers will care about your issue and opinion. As with all forms of public writing, it is important to make sure the readers are engaged and have a stake in your message.

Submit electronically: If possible, submit your op-ed via e-mail. This will ensure that it is received in a timely fashion. It is also helpful to use a publication's online commentary submission form (after you've drafted your submission using a word-processing tool, edited it and spell-checked it).

The Instructive Tip Sheet

The instructive tip sheet is a simple and concise list of "tips" or pointers that will help your target audiences with a particular need, task or situation. You've most likely seen them on television, in print and online.

- Ten Tips for Better Communications with Clients

- Top 12 Signs That Your Car Is a Lemon

- Six Surefire Ways to Avoid Legal Malpractice Lawsuits

- Top 10 Mistakes Employers Make in Their Employment Contracts

The ideas and topics are endless, but you need to know how to determine what will be effective for you and your firm.

NUMBERING YOUR TIP SHEETS

Tip sheets don't always need to be produced in lists of 10. It's acceptable to have less or more, but when you exceed 19, think about breaking the list into two lists of 10. If you surpass 25, then move to the section in this chapter that addresses writing a book.

As with all public relations tools, you need to have a plan and a purpose for your tip sheets. What do you want to write about and who do you want to reach? What are some of the questions that prospective clients frequently ask? What do your target audiences need to understand and how can you be more of a resource to them? Once you've answered these questions, then you need to determine which outlet will be most effective.

If you're trying to reach local consumers, you will be best served by reaching out to local newspapers and television news programs that run longer than one hour. If you are trying to reach corporate executives, you will want to target the print publications that they are most likely to read. For example, if you are trying to reach pharmaceutical companies' in-house counsel, think about which pharmaceutical and legal magazines they read rather that trying to pitch tips to *The Wall Street Journal* or *The New York Times*. The more focused you are, the more likely that your tips will be printed.

On the other hand, as a plaintiffs' attorney, it makes sense to author tip sheets that deal with ways to "protect yourself."

I recently consulted with a former workers' compensation judge-turned-claimants' attorney at Stampone D'Angelo Renzi DiPiero in Philadelphia and had him create the "Top 10 Things You Should Do If You Are Hurt or Exposed to Toxins at Work" *(see page 53)*. Here is that list, which has been republished with the firm's permission, and how we used it to successfully garner media coverage.

Once the tips were created, we had the tool we needed to pitch the media. In this case, our goal was to land a television interview on our local FOX affiliate during their morning program, knowing that it is a local consumer-watched show. After doing some research as to whom we should contact, we reached out to the producer who was responsible for guest appearances with one of the anchors and told her why we believed this would be an effective segment for their viewers. She liked the idea and booked our client, and he appeared on television shortly thereafter.

Two days before my client's appearance, we sent the producer the typed list and told her to feel free to republish the bullets on television during the segment and to use them on their Web site as long as proper attribution was given. This made her job even easier because she had more visuals to work with for the television segment. Remember, you have to think visual when you pitch to television producers.

Before the television appearance, we also sent an e-mail to the firm's clients and to contacts, family and friends, encouraging the readers to watch FOX29 "Good Day Philadelphia" on the date the show was to air.

If your office has heavy foot traffic, be sure to create an announcement and leave it in a highly visible area for others to see and pick up. Also make sure you leave copies in the general conference rooms.

PUTTING YOUR PEN TO PAPER

TOP 10 THINGS YOU SHOULD DO
IF YOU ARE HURT OR EXPOSED TO TOXINS AT WORK

10. Report the injury or exposure immediately to a supervisor or HR employee who is authorized to take an injury report, not a co-worker or team leader.

9. If necessary, seek immediate medical care. If you are still at work, ask your employer to provide the transportation.

8. If immediate medical care is not needed, consult with one of your employer's panel physicians as soon as possible. Panel physicians are frequently referred to as "company doctors."

7. Be certain to give to the physician a complete and accurate description of how the injury or exposure occurred and what injuries you have suffered.

6. Do not use your private or employer-provided health insurance. Tell the health care providers to bill your employer's workers' compensation insurance. If possible, get a claim number from the compensation carrier to provide if insurance information is needed.

5. Get the names, addresses and phone numbers of all eyewitnesses who saw what caused your injury.

4. Preserve physical evidence whenever possible, especially if a defective piece of machinery or equipment is involved. If you can, take photographs of the scene of the accident.

3. Write down the details of the event as soon as possible, while they are still fresh in your mind. Be thorough and accurate. This will help you to recall the event at a later date if necessary.

2. DO NOT SIGN ANYTHING except your witness or accident statement until you have consulted with your attorney.

And the most important advice that we can give you is this…

1. Be safety conscious. Keep alert for dangerous conditions around the workplace. When you discover a potentially dangerous condition, report it to your supervisor. Don't take unnecessary risks. Remember, the only good injury is the one that never happens.

After the show aired, the firm included the tips in its quarterly newsletter, added the tips to its Web site under the workers' compensation articles, and added it to the back of the printed biography for the workers' compensation practice description insert that goes along with the firm's brochure. These are all things you can do to maximize the value of your free publicity.

Here is an example of a tip sheet I wrote that explains how to maximize the use of tip sheets:

TEN SIMPLE TACTICS TO ADD VALUE TO YOUR TIP SHEET

1. Make tips available on your Web site.

2. Include tips in your corporate leave-behind.

3. Send tips to customers and prospects via e-mail.

4. Include tips in your corporate newsletter.

5. Create a tips postcard that can be sent to prospective clients.

6. Leave a copy of the tips in your lobby.

7. Create a link to the tips and include it in your e-mail signature.

8. Include a tips reprint in new-matter communications and allude to it in your cover letter.

9. Provide copies of your tips as a handout at seminars and trade shows.

10. Add copies of your tips to your media kit.

The Target-Centric Newsletter

Newsletters, done correctly, can be an effective part of your marketing efforts. Not only do newsletters display skills, talents and timely stories, they also can create buzz, open opportunities and bring in new business. No matter what type of newsletter you are producing, meaningful content is essential if you want it to be read. Here are some important things to consider:

PUTTING YOUR PEN TO PAPER

Since newsletters are niche publications, be sure to use a narrow focus and keep them specialized.

- Use timely, well-written stories about developments and trends that are important to your clients.

- Write stories from your clients' perspective, using appropriate jargon or explanations.

- Publish newsletters regularly.

- Humanize your stories. Stories about individuals are the most interesting.

- Customize your newsletter to make it stand out.

- E-mail is the fastest and cheapest way to get a newsletter out to your clients. However, e-mails can be mistaken for SPAM, so give the option of sending a hard copy through the mail. Also consider e-mail programs such as Constant Contact®.

- Put some thought into choosing your mailing lists.

When you stick to these guidelines, your newsletters can demonstrate expertise, establish credibility and create reader loyalty. These three aspects lead to trust, and a trusted company has power. The next time you're searching for an inexpensive way to boost your marketing efforts, consider a specialized client newsletter.

The Comprehensive Book

Most authors don't think of writing a book as a public relations tool. However, when you author a book, you can catapult your status from an average attorney to a well-known source for a particular subject. Indeed, writing and marketing a book is a colossal task. It means dedicating a great deal of time and resources in order to meet your goal. There are hundreds, if not thousands, of resources available regarding how to write and publish a book. Before you take on such a task, I highly recommend doing your homework.

FACT VS. FICTION

Now when I say "write a book," I'm referring to authoritative, industry-focused, factual publications, not fiction. Unless you truly believe you're the next Lisa Scottoline or John Grisham, then you should consider your topic carefully. According to Scottoline's Web site, when she decided to give writing a try, she was staying at home to be a mother. She lived a life solely financed by five Visa cards, and allowed herself five years or $50,000 in credit (whichever came first) to write and sell her first book. Three years later, she finished "Everywhere That Mary Went," her daughter started school and she had five maxed-out credit cards. Debt-ridden, Scottoline took a part-time job clerking for a federal appellate judge. No more than a week later, HarperCollins bought her now critically acclaimed first novel.

The Use of Publications to Promote Your Business

Each form of writing can be used to promote your business beyond the initial publication. The first thing you need to do is to review the publisher's copyright guidelines. These guidelines vary from one publisher to another.

Most publications will allow you to publish reprints. In the best-case scenario, you will be able to purchase a digital reprint which you will be permitted to upload on your Web site and distribute as you see fit—but these rights are rare. More frequently, you will be permitted to purchase printed reprints of the article, which you can then use to mail directly to your target audiences. Other ways to capitalize on your reprints:

- Add a link to the originating article on your firm's Web site and within your online biography.

- Include a link to your article in your e-mail signature.

- Leave copies of the article in the lobby of your office.

- Mail copies of the article to prospective and current clients.

- Send an e-mail to other attorneys who are good referral sources.

- Include the article with new business materials for prospective clients.

Other ways to capitalize on work you have already done include writing on essentially the same topic, but with a different angle or from a different perspective; incorporating portions of the material into speeches or presentations; and depending on the copyright, updating and resubmitting the piece to another publication at a later date.

Whatever you decide to submit for publication, remember that the time spent working on the material will pay off in spades. Putting pen to paper is always a worthwhile endeavor.

CHAPTER FIVE

> According to most studies, people's number
> one fear is public speaking. Number two is death.
> Death is number two. Does that sound right?
> This means to the average person, if you
> go to a funeral, you're better off in the
> casket than doing the eulogy.
> —*Jerry Seinfeld*

Speak Up and Be Heard

In addition to getting published to establish credibility and generate awareness, you can feed your interests while generating potential business by speaking at business forums, industry conferences, bar association meetings, seminars, universities and continuing legal-education programs. Ask yourself, "Do I enjoy speaking or presenting?" If the answer is yes, then ask yourself, "Who do I want to speak to?" Then go ahead and add speaking engagements to your publicity arsenal.

When you speak on a topic of interest, you are positioned as an expert in your field and can demonstrate rather than "sell" your knowledge, just like writing articles. Think back to the analogy of building the house.

Speaking engagements are just like hosting a housewarming party or wine and cheese. You are inviting people into your home to share something with them. In the case of a speaking engagement, it's your knowledge and how the attendees can leverage that knowledge to their advantage.

What to Say

Often attorneys are just as stumped for a speaking topic as they are for an article subject. If that's the case for you, go back to the previous chapter and revisit the ways we came up with topics to write about.

- Use "the FAQ Response Method," "the TOC Review Method," or "the Personal Experience Method" to determine your topic.

- Peruse magazines for trends, or create an outline of a speaking presentation from one of your tip sheets.

- Take what you've written about and use those same topics to create something valuable to say. For every article you write, you can create a topic to speak about and vice versa.

It's that easy.

TURNING PRESENTATIONS INTO ARTICLES

When you speak on a topic but haven't yet written an article on that same subject, tape-record your program and then have it transcribed. Voilà! You will have the first draft of an article.

Where to Say It

Another common concern among attorneys just getting into the speaking arena is that many are not sure where to speak. When looking for conferences to participate in, make sure the thought leaders in the industries that you serve will be present. This is no different than determining who you're going to invite to your housewarming party. Keep in mind that:

- Seminars should target prospective and current clients.

- Bar association speaking engagements and industry association conferences should target referral sources (i.e., attorneys who practice in different areas than you do).

- "How to" and "What You Should Know" programs should be used to target prospective consumer clients and can be presented as firm-sponsored community programs.

- "Ask the Attorney" programs and value-added programs can also be presented in partnership with local hospitals, community centers, senior centers and media outlets.

The locations and formats for your speaking engagements are endless if you are just a little bit creative.

If your seminar is open to the public or to a particular segment of the population, be sure to submit a calendar listing (see Chapter 8) to relevant publications that include such sections.

How to Say It

I have very rarely met an attorney who doesn't believe she is a great public speaker. And often, she is. But more often than not, the attorney went to law school to learn how to be a litigator. She knows how to argue a point, how to demonstrate a point in order to persuade the judge and jury, and how to negotiate. These are all great skills to possess, but they are not necessarily the same skills one needs to present in other venues.

Some of my favorite professors in law school were amazing litigators, but they also possessed the ability to teach and listen. Listening and responding is just as important in a speaking presentation as is your topic choice. If you fail to make a dynamic presentation, you will fail to impress your audiences. Remember those excruciatingly boring lectures you sat through in law school? Don't be that guy (or gal).

It's also important that you know the attendee demographics. Ask yourself, "Who is in attendance and what do they need from me?" Then prepare your program so that it is tailored to the attendees and meets their individual needs.

Once you know who your audience is and what its members need, it's important for you to determine the format and duration of your presentation. Personally, I don't care if you use PowerPoint® or a podium, flip charts or a digital whiteboard. What I do care about is that you don't rely on tools to deliver your presentation but rather use them to enhance it.

It is also very important to create branded handout materials that attendees can take away and use at their desks. Don't just hand out your firm's brochure and your business card. That's just as bad as the speaker who says, "If you'd like more information, give me your business card, and I'll send you the handout." It may be a great sales and lead-generation tool, but it's not an effective way to build credibility.

The handout should be something that has shelf-life: a checklist, a case update, a list of resources, etc. It should always be printed on, at the very least, firm letterhead, with your name, direct telephone number and e-mail address.

SHOULD SEMINAR ATTENDEES PAY TO PLAY?

The question of whether seminar attendees should pay to play is one that has been debated by legal communicators for many years. Some believe that for seminars to be successful communications tools, you should never charge a fee. Others believe that the more you charge, the more value the attendees perceive and the more likely they are to show up. On one hand, charging a fee does help to defray costs, but on the other hand, it can also create a logistical accounting nightmare. My experience and research indicate that most firms have moved away from the pay-to-play model. Ultimately, if you want the seminar to result in new business, then what's most important is that those who are likely to purchase your services are in attendance and that you deliver something of value. Finally, you will need to follow up effectively.

How to Leverage What You've Said

Once your presentation is complete, be sure to stay afterward to field questions and have additional conversations with the attendees. Make sure you send every attendee a thank-you letter for attending your program and include additional information that may be helpful. Then, take special time to follow up with those who expressed interest in learning more about you or your firm or those who expressed a concern about a specific matter. Be careful not to overtly "solicit" their business, but rather, get to know how you can help them and let them know how to reach you if they have a need.

CHAPTER SIX

> There are events which are so great that
> if a writer has participated in them his obligation
> is to write truly rather than assume the
> presumption of altering them with invention.
> —*Ernest Hemingway*

Special Events That Get Attention

Earlier in the book, I defined public relations as the art and science of proactive advocacy on the part of a company, individual or brand. I said it requires strategic management of your position statement and key messages in order to reach your target audiences and, through various tactics, establish goodwill and a mutual understanding. This means that we must not only rely on media relations, but we must create programs that build relationships with our target audiences and the community. Examples of ways to do this include:

- Celebrate a holiday or anniversary.
- Conduct a poll or survey.
- Create a contest.
- Educate a consumer audience.
- Sponsor an art exhibit.

- Issue a research-based report.
- Make an analysis or prediction.
- Partner with a nonprofit.
- Perform pro bono work.

Getting Involved in the Community

In the current day and age, community relations are of growing importance to law firms. Because society expects corporations to be socially responsible, becoming active in the community is to everyone's advantage.

Community relations is the task of establishing a connection with the community and raising and maintaining the firm's general public profile. Community relations activities can include exhibitions, celebrations, ceremonies, speeches, sponsorship of nonprofit organizations, pro bono work, official representation at functions and participation in community activities.

Such programs are mutually beneficial to both the community and the law firm. From the firm's side, a good corporate neighbor policy improves internal morale and assists with the recruitment and retention of staff and attorneys. From the community's perspective, the organization's actions demonstrate the firm's dedication to its target audiences and the public. When information about the programs is publicized, it generates goodwill and reinforces your corporate brand.

Special Events: Planning for Success

The benefits of an open house celebration or a holiday soiree for your organization can be abundant. They introduce your business as an important player in the community and serve as a vehicle to connect with your publics. Planning and consideration are the keys to long-term success.

Like any communication to your target audiences, a holiday open house, for instance, is a public relations event. Know why you are hosting such a party and who should attend. Ask yourself, "What do I want each attendee to walk away remembering about this company?" The preparation and thought you invest will undoubtedly determine whether your event is a success. Document your plan and checklist so that you create a system for duplication each year.

SPECIAL EVENTS THAT GET ATTENTION

EVENT-PLANNING CHECKLIST

_____ Theme
_____ Special guest/s
_____ Location, date, time and duration
_____ Guest list
_____ Save-the-date cards (if necessary)
_____ Invitations and directions
_____ Entertainment
_____ Catering and rental needs
_____ Decorations
_____ Sound system
_____ Parking
_____ Presentation and announcements
_____ Tours (if located in your office)
_____ Favors
_____ Follow-up

Setting a date is the first step. If your open house is any time in December, set the date early and send save-the-date cards. It is also helpful to have a New Year event in January in order to avoid December overload.

Make sure the time for your open house is convenient for clients, employees, the media and potential clients. If you are having a special guest, dignitary or entertainment as part of the festivities, determine that person's availability before you set the date. Also allow sufficient time for obtaining vendors and delivering invitations.

Invitations should be customized, concise and memorable. Contact potential vendors and request quotes and samples. Hire an illustrator to customize an invitation that captures the flavor of your business, brand, industry or work environment. Send your invitations at least six weeks prior to the big event. Remember to save your invitation list from year to year. If you do it right, you will need to do it again. That means inviting the same people each year. Otherwise, you can count on the caller who says, "Are you having your open house again this year? I didn't get an invitation and want to make sure it's on my calendar..."

Invite your sphere of influence: current clients, business contacts, referral sources and your media contacts. Friends and family also add value to the attendee list. Use membership lists from civic organizations, trade associations, professional affiliates and governmental agencies to further develop your list. Your guest list should include a significant number of invitees to ensure a good turnout—especially if your event is close to any holiday in November or December. The average response rate for most functions is less than 20 percent.

The media can be an important part of your invitee list. Keep it simple. Only invite a few key members of the media with whom you have existing relationships. You don't want to patronize them, as this is not an enticement for coverage. Don't expect news coverage from the event. This is a relationship-building time for you and your media contacts, so make that clear.

Decorations, entertainment and refreshments are all crucial details when planning your event. Decorations should be appropriate. Select a theme or color scheme that reflects your brand. Make sure the decorations are not elaborate, just simple and effective. Forget the balloons altogether: they're great for a kid's birthday party, so leave them there.

When it comes to entertainment, music can add a nice touch to any event. Consider the mood that you would like to set. Do you want a DJ, strolling minstrels, a background pianist or an acoustic guitarist? It all depends on the type of party you are planning, so decide accordingly. Be sure to consider a sound system for the few short announcements and thank-you messages you will deliver to your guests.

As for the refreshments, that should be determined by the number of attendees, the mood of the event and the time of day. If your event will be held during a major mealtime, refreshments should be more substantial. Make sure there is something there for everyone. We live in a time of great diversity and healthy choices. Be sure to include vegetarian and vegan alternatives, and peanut- and shellfish-free dishes. If you're inviting your colleagues with their families, include one or two child-friendly options.

Finally, think about the take-away. Why are you inviting people to attend your event? Personally, I'm not in favor of handouts, brochures, trinkets or other such giveaways at a celebration. This is a goodwill event, so let the invitation and the event be the take-away. If you make it memorable, people will want to attend year after year. On the other hand, if you are so inclined to spend the money on favors, make sure they leave a lasting impact. Think about the item that will remain long after the party is over. What fits within the theme of your gathering and still makes sense for you to give to your attendees? There is no one single answer—it all depends on your firm's culture, its budget and what will hit a home run with your guests.

Provided that you approach your gathering as a public relations tool and plan accordingly, you should be able to promote your practice by building and reinforcing relationships with your target audiences. You just might have a good time in the process!

CHAPTER SEVEN

Life isn't about finding yourself.
Life is about creating yourself.
—*Ernest Hemingway*

Recognize
and Be Recognized

Awards programs are excellent public relations tools to enable you to recognize and be recognized. There are two ways to implement awards programs to build your business: 1) Apply for awards for which you qualify; and 2) Create awards for your target audiences.

APPLYING FOR AWARDS

There are many awards for which your law firm or individual attorneys might qualify. Look to your local business journal, chambers of commerce, trade publications and bar associations to start. Many of these outlets conduct pro bono service, women-in-business, and young executive/attorney awards each year.

You should also check national trade publications and the American Bar Association for additional awards opportunities.

Apply for awards that recognize community service, pro

bono work, Web sites, firm marketing and public relations, diversity, and anything else for which your firm or its attorneys stand out. Be sure to set aside a budget line each year for awards applications, as they can become quite expensive.

Create a system to track the awards that you apply for each year. Track the name of the sponsoring organization and all of its contact information, the early-application and final-application deadlines, the criteria for application, the application fee, your firm's submissions, and the results of your submissions. You can then use this system to manage your awards-application program from year to year, which will ultimately save you time and money.

When your firm or one of its attorneys receives an award, you will want to let others know about it. It's not enough just to receive an award. That's like building a house but never inviting anyone over for coffee.

When you receive an award, you should do all of the following:

- Write a press release surrounding each award.

- Add the press release to your Web site.

- Include the award information in your firm's newsletter.

- Add a link in your attorneys' e-mail signatures to the award information on your Web site.

- Send the press release along with the appropriate head shots (with captions) to your local media and bar publications.

- Leave copies of your press releases in your firm's lobby and conference and meeting areas.

If you don't have a firm newsletter, write a letter to your clients and prospects. Include pertinent legal information and announce the news of your award and how this benefits the people to whom you're sending the letter.

RECOGNIZE AND BE RECOGNIZED

A great example of a law firm Web site that includes "Awards and Honors" used to support the firm's marketing and public relations initiatives is that of Jenner & Block LLP, which can be found at www.jenner.com.

AWARDS VS. DIRECTORIES

Awards are not the same as directories, Web sites and organizations that rank attorneys and law firms. A partial list of such publications includes:

- American Lawyer AMLaw 200
- Best Lawyers in America
- Chambers Global
- Chambers UK
- Chambers USA
- Euromoney Expert Guides
- Global 100
- Lawdragon 500 and Lawdragon 3000
- Leading Lawyers
- Legal 500 United States
- Legal Experts
- Martindale-Hubbell
- Multicultural Law Top 100
- National Law Journal 250
- Of Counsel 700
- PLC Which Lawyer? Yearbook
- SuperLawyers
- UK Legal 500
- US Legal 500
- The Vault
- Who's Who Legal

For more comprehensive lists, read Leigh Dance's *Global Guide to Law Firm and Lawyer Directories* and the companion book compiled by Deborah McMurray, *North American Guide to Law Firm and Lawyer Directories.*

Creating Awards for Your Target Audiences

The premise of an awards program is to celebrate those companies and individuals who exemplify the characteristics that resonate with your firm's culture. Awards programs should also have meaning and be created because your firm has something to say.

Even the name of the award is extremely important, as it needs to reinforce your firm's brand and still be unique in and of itself. When creating an award, think about what you want it to accomplish. Ask yourself:

- Are we trying to reach a particular niche industry or market segment?

- Are there any prominent figureheads in our industry or firm for whom the award should be named?

- Is there a unique innovation, program or methodology that has helped people, the community or target industry that can be acknowledged?

- What are the criteria that will demonstrate the characteristics of the award?

- And finally, what exactly is the award? Does it have monetary value? Is it a donation to the awardees' charities of choice? Is it pro bono service for a year to a nonprofit?

One example of a successful awards program is that of White & Williams LLP in Philadelphia. This firm created the White & Williams Virginia Barton Wallace Award in 2006. The award honors Virginia "Ginny" Barton Wallace, their first female partner, who passed away in 2002.

According to Robin Nolan, the firm's Marketing Director: "Our goal in establishing the award was to focus on women leaders in business and in law. So now, we honor Ginny's memory and her contribution to women in law while reaching a strategic audience of corporate women thought leaders and decision makers." The award includes a $10,000 check, which is presented to a charity of the recipient's choice.

Once you decide on the award itself, it will be necessary to determine whether you will choose the award recipient without seeking applicants or conduct media relations and advertising to seek qualified applicants. If you do seek applicants, you will also need to organize a qualified pool of judges.

Finally, you will need to organize an event to which you can invite clients, prospects, referral sources, employees and industry thought leaders. Once the recipient is determined, pre- and post-event publicity (media relations) should be executed.

PART TWO
THE TOOLS
OF THE TRADE

CHAPTER EIGHT

" If one cannot state a matter clearly enough so that
even an intelligent 12-year-old can understand it,
one should remain within the cloistered walls
of the university and laboratory until one gets
a better grasp of one's subject matter. "

—*Margaret Mead*

Media
Outreach Tools

Media relations is the process of reaching out to the decision makers within media outlets to garner inclusion
in a story (media coverage). Newspapers, magazines,
Web sites, television programs, Internet media outlets
and radio shows have large amounts of space and time
to fill and depend upon publicists and other individuals
to help provide story ideas, interview subjects, background information and other material.

When you conduct media relations, you need to pitch
your idea to the reporter, editor or producer of your
desired publication or program.

Pitching is the art of communicating a story idea, guest
speaker or news item to the media in order to gain

publicity. The pitch can come in the form of a mailed letter, e-mail, a telephone conversation or voicemail (though I prefer to avoid voicemail for pitches).

In Chapter 3, we talked about the best ways to communicate with the media, including the art of pitching. In this chapter, we will focus on the different tools you can use to reach the media. These include press releases, media advisories, backgrounders, press kits and more. We'll also address how you can use these same tools to reach other target audiences in your everyday public relations efforts.

In order to most effectively pitch your news and story ideas to the media, you need to become familiar with several media outreach tools, including the press release, media photo, backgrounder, question-and-answer document, media advisory and press kit.

The Press Release

A press release is a crucial public relations tool that can be used in a variety of ways. You may read countless articles and online commentaries that say the press release is dead, but that's a bunch of malarkey.

The press release is still one of the most commonly used tools to solidify your message and get it out there via various forms of outreach. It also helps you to develop your key messages and ensure that everyone in your firm agrees to the language you plan to use to communicate your message.

Also known as a news release, a press release is a concise news vehicle that is most commonly provided to the media in order to generate public awareness and interest about a story or piece of news. It should convey the "who, what, when, where, why and how" of your story. It is the written communiqué designed to present the most newsworthy or attention-grabbing aspect of the story you are pitching.

A pseudo news story, the press release should be written in the third person and should demonstrate to an editor or reporter the newsworthiness of a particular person, event, service or story you are trying to communicate. Please do not take the word "newsworthy" lightly. This is one of the biggest mistakes attorneys make. Not everything is newsworthy. Really. The fact that you settled a negligence case for $50,000 prearbitration really doesn't hold much interest for those not involved in the matter. Now, if you settled a wrongful death case for $7.5 million that is not confidential, and you can name the defendants, there might be a story.

Press releases typically follow certain industry guidelines to help the media identify and clarify who you are, what your story is about and how they can contact you for more information.

USING THE PRESS RELEASE FOR BUSINESS DEVELOPMENT

Even though the press release is typically used to garner media attention and attain press coverage, it can also be used to create a buzz, generate awareness and develop business. In addition to remaining in the eyes of the media positively and consistently, you need to communicate your messages to clients, prospects, colleagues, friends, family and referral sources. The more often these audiences hear your firm name, the more likely they will remember your firm when they need legal services. Some great ways to use a press release besides sending it to the media include:

- Send it to current and prospective clients, vendors, referral sources, family and friends as "Firm News."
- Include it on your firm Web site.
- Send it to all of your firm's employees via e-mail and encourage them to pass the news along to their contacts.
- Include the press release on your firm's intranet.
- Make copies of the press release and leave them in your office and your lobby.
- Include copies of your more-important press releases in your firm's press kit, newsletters and leave-behinds.
- Have extra copies of your news releases available to attendees of your seminars and at your trade show booths.

Whatever the news, there are many ways to use a press release to increase awareness of your firm and its offerings, sell your services, retain current clients and generate new business.

It is also important to know when you should issue press releases. Situations that usually warrant the use of a press release include: new business wins, new hires, speaking engagements, seminars, CLE's, awards, board appointments, substantial or newsworthy verdicts, resolutions or settlements (nonconfidential), mergers and acquisitions, marketing initiatives, nonprofit or pro bono involvement, and much more. Just see what your target media outlets are reporting on, and you'll know if they might be interested in your story.

Writing the Press Release

Many factors go into writing a good press release and will influence the amount and type of coverage your item will receive. It is important to follow a number of rules so that your communications are effective.

> **Include the date and time your news is to be released:** It is important that the recipient of your press release understands the time sensitivity of your news. You must tell the reporter when to disseminate the information. Common language to provide this information includes: For Immediate Release, For Release Before [Date], or For Release After [Date]. This language should appear at the top of the press release and be either all caps, underlined or bolded. You should also include a dateline in bold. The dateline is listed at the beginning of the first paragraph with the city, state abbreviation and date of the news's origin. For example: Philadelphia, Pa. (June 12, 2010).

STATE ABBREVIATIONS

There are two stylebooks most common to writing public relations materials. They are *The Chicago Manual of Style* and *The Associated Press Stylebook and Libel Manual.* Each provides recommendations for writing styles that are most commonly used in the news industry. Throughout this book, we will defer to AP style since this manual seems to serve as the bible of the journalism industry. The AP uses multiletter abbreviations for most states but does not abbreviate Alaska, Hawaii, Idaho, Iowa, Maine, Ohio, Texas or Utah. Examples include: Alabama (Ala.), Connecticut (Conn.), Washington, D.C. (D.C.), Massachusetts (Mass.), New York (N.Y.) Oklahoma (Okla.) and Pennsylvania (Pa.)—certainly not what I remember from 3rd-grade letter writing.

Include contact information: It is extremely irritating to a reporter or editor to receive an interesting press release but have no idea where it came from. You should therefore make sure that, if you mail your press release, you have printed it on letterhead and included contact information for yourself or your firm's marketing or public relations manager. If you send it via e-mail, place the appropriate contact name, business phone number, cell phone number and e-mail address at the top of the page.

Include a creative headline: A creative and clever headline is important. The headline must be catchy in order to entice recipients to read your release.

A good way to come up with headline ideas is to read the headlines featured in newspapers, magazines, blogs and any other media outlets you are trying to target. Headlines are meant to tell the story and catch the reader's attention in just a few short words. In the same way, the subject line of an e-mail needs to be short, compelling and descriptive. Think of your headline as your e-mail subject line—does it grab the recipient's attention? Of course, oftentimes the headline is what it is. Let us use the example of attorney Jane P. Doe, who joins the Philadelphia, Pa., law firm of Buck & Fawn P.C. as a partner in its insurance defense litigation practice. How creative can the headline really be? For example, the headline should read something like this: "Doe Joins Philadelphia's Buck & Fawn as Litigation Partner."

Tailor the headline to the outlet: It is also important to tailor your headline to each outlet so the outlet knows why your story pertains to it or its audiences. Assume Jane Doe is a member of the American Bar Association. The release sent to the editor of its internal newsletter or member publication should have a headline reading "American Bar Member, Doe, Joins Buck & Fawn as Litigation Partner." The same holds true for alumni publications, newspapers from the town where Jane resides and other affinity organization publications.

Include a subheadline if it will add value: A "subhead" can be an extremely useful tool when used properly, but it is often over-looked. The press release subhead provides an opportunity for you to incorporate your news angle and further catch the reporter's attention without taking away from the headline. In the case of Jane Doe, assume she is a lateral hire and left another prominent national law firm, Gelding & Mare. The subhead could read: "Doe Leaves Gelding & Mare to Head Buck & Fawn's Insurance Defense Practice."

Provide the news value: You must tie your press release topic into the news. Come up with story angles that will be of interest to reporters, and tell them why their readers will care about this information and how the story will be beneficial to them. If your press release is just informational, keep it short. For example, if you are pitching your local business journal, the news has to be of value to business readers. Ask yourself why a reader would care about your story. Then, use your answer to craft a sentence or two about the news value of your story and how it relates to the business industry regionally.

Summarize the release in the first paragraph: Also known as the press release "lead," the first paragraph should allow the reporter to determine what the release is all about. Get straight to the point. The first paragraph should answer who, what, when, where and why. Put it this way so that if the reporter is crunched for time, she can include just the basics of your story in a news item. Make it easy for her to do that. For example, many local newspapers include blurbs about local business news without getting into detail. If the first paragraph of your press release says: "Jane P. Doe, Esq., recently joined the law firm of Buck & Fawn P.C. as a partner heading the insurance defense litigation practice. Doe will work from the firm's headquarters in Philadelphia, Pa.," and just that much got printed, the most important items would be covered. It would certainly be nice if the story included Jane's experience, her previous law firm, some of the clients she has worked with in the past, her alma maters, her media appearances and any publications; but if it does not, that is okay, too.

Keep it short and concise: Typically, a press release should be no more than two pages. One page is preferable. That means you should not be writing a legal treatise or brief—it's a press release. Stick to the facts. Use only enough words to tell your story. Publications have space restrictions and may need to cut off the last paragraph of your story. Therefore, make sure you have the most important information first, followed by more details that may be interesting but are not crucial. Always be sure to write clearly, using proper grammar and spelling.

Avoid jargon and excessive adjectives: The reader is not looking for fluff, and, unless you are writing to a legally trained reporter, the use of legalese can muddy the waters. Also steer clear of unnecessary adjectives, fancy language or superfluous expressions such as "superior services" or "extremely experienced and qualified." This type of language raises red flags as fluff with a reporter and can get you into trouble with your state's ethics board.

Check your facts: Make sure that your facts are correct. If you send a reporter incorrect information, you can forget about ever appearing in her media outlet again. That said, if you made a mistake in your facts or if the facts changed along the way, let the reporter know—just own up to it. It's a basic fact of life that things change. If you are up front about it, you can minimize any potential damage. It is also good to include statistics whenever appropriate and possible, depending on the type of story and if the statistics will enhance it in any way.

Include a quote: Quotes help to make the press release more personal and add value to the communiqué. Some publications will never run quotes unless they have been personally verified by a reporter or editor at the publication. This holds true for most of the national and trade print publications. However, many local newspapers will run your press release verbatim. Your press release should also be added to your firm's Web site and issued to online sources, all of which will likely include the quote. Continuing with the Jane

Doe story, a valuable quote would come from the hiring or managing partner of Buck & Fawn P.C. explaining why Jane was hired, the value she brings to the firm and how this benefits the firm's clients.

Use names in your release: Always be sure to include the most important people in your news story. Write out the person's full name and title on first reference in the release. So, when we speak of Jane Doe for the first time, we would say, "Jane P. Doe, Esq." When we refer to Jane after that, we refer to her by last name only: "Doe." We do not use "Ms. Doe" or "Mrs. Doe" or "Jane."

Using only the last name is not the case when writing biographies for your firm's Web site or client communications. These name references will depend upon your firm's culture, the types of clients you serve and how previous materials have been written (for consistency purposes).

Indicate that there are no more pages to the release: After the main body of the release, skip a line and in the center type three or five number signs (### or #####) or the number 30 with a dash on each side of it (–30–). This end notation lets the reporter know that there are no more pages to the release when printed. Does this sound archaic? Yes. Is it absolutely necessary? No. Why, then, is it convention? The answer: strictly because some people still use arcane methods to receive press releases (such as the facsimile machine), and, therefore, it is important for the recipient to know when the final page has arrived.

Include a boilerplate: A boilerplate is the standard block of text that is used at the end of every release. Your firm's boilerplate should be consistent and used for all press releases. The boilerplate should contain a brief description of your firm. For example, Buck & Fawn's boilerplate might read something like this:

Buck & Fawn P.C. is a national law firm of more than 1,000 attorneys specializing in civil defense litigation. Founded in 1920, Buck & Fawn is headquartered in Philadelphia, Pa., and maintains additional offices in Akron, Ohio; New York, N.Y.; Wilmington, Del.; and Los Angeles, Calif. Buck & Fawn has successfully defended clients ranging from Fortune 500 companies to local sole proprietors. Capabilities include insurance defense, employment matters, contract disputes and SEC litigation. For additional information, please see Buck & Fawn's Web site, www.BuckFawnLaw.com.

Research the intended recipient of your press release: Before sending a release to the media, research the reporter or editor you are targeting. Make sure that he or she is the correct person to receive the release. You can go to the outlet's Web site, use a paid media database source *(see page 24)* or pick up the phone and call the publication to ask. Also, it cannot hurt to find out how the reporter or editor prefers to receive press releases—via fax, e-mail or snail mail.

A Press Release Checklist

Remember to ask yourself whether your press release is newsworthy, factual and accurate. Is it short and concise? Also be sure to check that you have included the following:

_____ Dateline and Release line
_____ Contact information
_____ Headline
_____ Subhead (optional)
_____ Personalized information for each media outlet
_____ Who
_____ What
_____ When
_____ Where
_____ Why
_____ How
_____ Quote (optional)
_____ End notation
_____ Boilerplate

SAMPLE PRESS RELEASE

Assume Jane Doe of Buck & Fawn recently addressed medical malpractice defense issues at a Pennsylvania health care summit. The firm would like insurance companies, medical providers and in-house counsel from health care institutions to know that Jane is knowledgeable and passionate about these issues. Therefore, the firm is going to issue a "post-event" press release to leverage the media attention it will garner. Here is what that press release might look like:

FOR IMMEDIATE RELEASE

Buck & Fawn P.C. Attorneys at Law

Contact: Judy Smith, Communications Director
215.555.0212 or judysmith@buckfawnlaw.com

Doctors Leaving PA - Medical Malpractice Lawsuits Must Be Capped

Insurance Defense Lawyer Will Address the Current State of
Malpractice Liability Insurance in Pennsylvania for Insurance Companies,
Medical Providers and Health Care Institutions

Philadelphia, Pa., August 10, 2009–Earlier today, Jane Doe, Esq., Partner, Buck & Fawn P.C., met with Gov. Edwin D. Roobell and other state officials and industry leaders to examine the current availability and cost of medical malpractice liability insurance for physicians in Pennsylvania. Doe provided a defense attorney's perspective on these issues, stating that "medical malpractice lawsuits must be capped because doctors are leaving Pennsylvania in droves."

Pennsylvania's medical malpractice insurance industry has been in a state of flux for the past decade. As headlines warn that physicians are leaving the state due to the increasing cost of malpractice insurance, opponents of tort reform contend that the situation is not as dire as it appears. Recently, a major charitable organization completed an in-depth study into the state of malpractice liability insurance in Pennsylvania. Government officials and industry leaders are now poised to examine the results of this research endeavor and chart a path designed to benefit health care consumers and physicians.

Doe highlighted that physicians are leaving Pennsylvania at an alarming rate due to the high prevalence of medical malpractice lawsuits and soaring insurance costs. Physicians in eastern Pennsylvania have also seen their annual malpractice premiums more than double, in some cases to over $100,000 per doctor.

The discussion at the Harrisburg Government Building was heated.

Doe has been representing insurance providers and insureds for more than two decades. She recently joined leading defense firm Buck & Fawn P.C. as a partner in the Insurance Defense Litigation Group. Notably, Doe successfully represented a major hospital in a $5 million medical malpractice matter where she was able to prove that a plastic surgery patient had a pre-existing condition that led to his death.

Buck & Fawn P.C. is a national law firm of more than 1,000 lawyers specializing in civil defense litigation. Founded in 1920, Buck & Fawn is headquartered in Philadelphia, Pa., and maintains additional offices in Akron, Ohio; New York, N.Y.; Wilmington, Del.; and Los Angeles, Calif. Buck & Fawn has successfully defended clients ranging from Fortune 500 companies to local sole proprietors. Capabilities include insurance defense, employment matters, contract disputes and SEC litigation. For additional information, please see Buck & Fawn's Web site, www.BuckFawnLaw.com.

WIRE DISTRIBUTION OF PRESS RELEASES

In Chapter 3, we learned how to put the media to work for you and how to pitch the media. There are additional tools called wire services that you should be familiar with. First, understand that wire services, both paid and free, serve the purpose of providing the media with information that they've requested on certain topics; however, unless you're a very large organization, or your news is extraordinary, using a wire service is not likely to get your story covered. However, it will help get your firm's story out on the Internet and onto Web sites that pull their news from the wires. The wire services available to you include:

- Associated Press (AP.org)
- Black PR Wire (Blackprwire.com)
- Business Wire (Businesswire.com)
- Dow Jones Newswires (Djnewswires.com)
- E News Wires (Enewswires.com)
- Hispanic PR Wire (Hispanicprwire.com)
- Marketwire (Marketwire.com)
- Medialink (Medialink.com)

- NAPS (Napsnet.com)
- PrimeNewswire (Primenewswire.com)
- PR Newswire (Prnewswire.com)
- PR Web (Prweb.com)
- Reuters (Reuters.com)
- U.S. Asian Wire (Usasianwire.com)
- Vocus (Vocus.com)

The Media Photo

In many cases, including a photo or two with a press release can add greater impact and news value to your story, not only for the readers of the publication (if it gets picked up), but also for the editor when deciding which stories to cover. If you have a **good** photo of a person or event that you can attach to a release, you should do so. It will not hurt your chances of getting coverage—it can only help.

There are many reasons to include photos that illustrate the news in your press release. A press release with a photo attached is four times more likely to be read. Small publications generally like to receive photos with press releases because it enables them to publish photos without having to send a photographer or reporter to take pictures. Larger publications also like to receive photos because, in addition to adding interest to a story, photos help the writer authenticate the story or event to her editor.

Head shots are frequently used to illustrate the individual or individuals featured in a news story. Public relations practitioners often send them to television stations when pitching clients for an appearance, and we always include them with news articles about individuals.

A great head shot can be very beneficial. It can say, "I am approachable, I am trustworthy, and I am a good person to work with." A bad head shot can say, "I do not care what you think of me," or "I am too cheap to invest in myself or my firm."

So, the first piece of advice is to put your own digital camera away and invest in yourself. Good up-to-date head shots are important to keep on file, and they have a shelf life of four to eight years (depending on how often you change your hairstyle). If your head shot is more than eight years old, it's time to ante up and reinvest.

A photo shoot can be a fruitless venture if you're not properly prepared, however. Here are some easy steps to follow to ensure a smooth photo shoot and a desirable result:

- **Show expression:** Let your eyes do the talking. Smile when it is appropriate. Use your body language to express your sentiment.

- **Be versatile:** Your head shot needs to appeal to many different audiences.

- **The focus is on you, not on what you're wearing:** Wear simple, solid-colored clothing. Avoid patterns or wearing all one color. Layering with a collared shirt or jacket allows you to look professional and vary your look easily from shot to shot. Refrain from wearing bulky jewelry or accessories that will take the spotlight off of your face.

- **Show your "everyday" self:** Wear your hair and makeup as you typically would any day of the week.

- **Expect that the shoot will take one to two hours:** Allow plenty of time so that you are not rushed or stressed.

- **Remember that the photographer is a professional:** This person will use her skills and experience to create the best photos for your needs.

- **Practice your facial expressions** (smile, no smile, teeth showing, serious, etc.) in a mirror.

- **Have several shirt and jacket options** and bring them all with you on the day of the shoot.

- **Get plenty of sleep** the night before the shoot.

- **Engage a hair stylist and makeup professional** so you look your best.

- **Relax and have fun!** Your picture will reflect that.

The Nitty Gritty on Photos

When it comes time for you to get your head shot taken, remember that it does not have to be a stressful undertaking. Just arrive prepared and be yourself. If you do your part, the professionals involved can easily create some pleasing visuals for you. There are also a few rules that you should follow when using photos to tell your story.

As already indicated, a head shot illustrates one person. However, it is often necessary to send a photo that captures an event or illustrates your case. When you send event photos, make sure you know the editors' preferences. I know one newspaper editor who greatly dislikes staged shots such as the so-called "grip and grin," giant check donations, or several people facing the camera and saying "cheese." She would rather receive candid shots taken in the style of photojournalism. Other publications—especially trade journals and business journals—will want you to send the standard business photos.

Give your photo a descriptive name: First and foremost, if you plan to send the photo digitally, make sure the name of the image depicts exactly who or what it is. So for example, if you are sending a head shot of attorney Jane Doe, you will want to name the photo "JaneDoeEsq." If you send "IMG_001," then there is no way for the editor to remember that "IMG_001" is a photo of Jane Doe, especially if the photo is forwarded on to another person at the publication.

Include a descriptive caption: If you are sending a photo, include a descriptive "photo caption" following the boilerplate and including the subject of the photo, the names and titles of the people in the photo, and where it was taken. If you need to credit the photographer, add her name and contact information. Also remember that, since we read from left to right, your photo caption should (if depicting people) state, "From L to R: Name 1, Name 2, Name 3," and so on.

Write captions on the backs of printed photos: If you are mailing a photo, do not forget to include a caption on the back, especially if you are sending more than one photo.

If you cannot send a photo to every publication, then just send one to those you feel are most likely to incorporate it. Then, for the other publications, include a line at the bottom of the release stating that a photo is available upon request.

TIPS FOR SENDING DIGITAL PHOTOGRAPHS

Most publications require 300 dpi, 5 x 7 digital photographs. Make sure to use a universal format like JPEG or TIF.

Title the photo in its digital format. Do not have it saved as "DVR_0001" or whatever format your camera saves in when downloading to your computer.

Use the name of your company, event or the person pictured to save the photo.

Make sure before you e-mail it that the editor or reporter accepts attachments, as many SPAM filters and antivirus programs reject attachments.

Use online photo galleries when possible: If your office is able to upload photos to the firm Web site, you can include a link to the photo page at the end of your press releases. This is a great way to share captioned photos with the media because it allows them to choose which photos best illustrate your story. They should also be given the choice to download high- or low-resolution copies of the photos for use with their publications.

If your firm does not have the ability to upload photos and captions, use an online digital photo site such as shutterfly.com, flickr.com, myphotosharing.com or kodakgallery.com. Although the media will not always be able to download a digital file from these sites, they will be able to tell you which photos they would like you to send. This form of communication should be used carefully, as it adds more work for the reporter. But if you have a good relationship with a reporter, she will likely want to look at the photos and make her own choices. Be sure to take the time to include information about each photo (names, places, dates, etc.) on the site.

The Backgrounder

Backgrounders serve many purposes. Their primary purpose is to provide in-depth background information about a company, person, place or story. In the case of legal communications, they should provide background on your firm, its attorneys and the news you are disseminating.

The hallmarks of a good backgrounder are accuracy, conciseness and comprehensiveness. Backgrounders serve to introduce the firm, a practitioner, a news item, nonlegal experts, practice areas, service offerings (such as seminars and continuing legal education programs), and the management team. They also make it clear why you are contacting members of the media.

Public relations practitioners use backgrounders as brief documents that provide reporters, editors and interviewers with enough information on a subject to conduct a thoughtful and intelligent interview. They also provide information that would be used in a press release, but for the fact that the release needs to be shorter and more concise. The backgrounder, although still written in the third person, need not be short. That said, this is not a license to create literary masterpieces 10 pages in length.

Usually not more than a few pages (two to five), the backgrounder is also used to answer any anticipated questions about a particular subject. The more information you provide initially, the more prepared you will be when the media calls. This is especially true when dealing with complex legal issues and matters that have been the focus of media scrutiny. The backgrounder, when used, often accompanies a press release. Accordingly, there are some basic rules you should abide by:

> **Repeat your concise statement of the issue:** The statement of the issue that is the subject of your press release should be repeated as your opening statement.

Provide an historical overview: Follow the opening with an historical overview of the matter. Keep it tight and organize it either chronologically or in another order that will make sense to the reader. Describe the story's evolution—give it perspective. How did it start and what were the major events leading up to its conclusion or resolution?

Cite your sources: If you refer to other materials, books, Web sites or news items, be sure to cite your sources.

Include other thought leaders: A backgrounder is used to provide just that: background. Such information also includes additional sources for a complete story. For example, let's say Jane Doe just completed a U.S. Supreme Court appellate argument regarding a case of first impression, which resulted in a favorable outcome for an insurance provider. Jane's backgrounder should not only detail the issues but also should provide the name and contact information of the insurance company's spokesperson, insurance industry experts and, if appropriate, opposing counsel and perhaps other attorneys who might add depth to the reporter's story.

Provide relevancy: Explain why the issue you're highlighting is important today. Ask yourself: "What is the significance? Why does this matter today? Who cares?" Then, back up your relevancy statement with facts.

Include the attorney's experience: Rather than clutter the press release with a full-page biography about Jane Doe, include her full biography in the backgrounder. This is a great place to list Jane's involvement in other cases that add depth to the issue at hand.

Include a firm overview: It is important to remember to include an overview of your firm. No matter the size of your organization, there is a firm behind you, even in the case of the sole practitioner. It is therefore important to include an overview to provide perspective, even if it is identical to your Web site "about us" information.

Organize your backgrounder with subheadings: Use subheads where appropriate to organize your information and make it easier to read. Based on the tips provided here, your subheads should include: Issues, Historical Overview, Relevancy and Facts, Additional Sources/ Commentators, Attorney Biography and Firm Overview.

The Opinion Editorial

As we saw in Chapter 4, an op-ed (opinion-editorial) is a form of writing that is used to express a personal opinion. It is an underutilized and extremely powerful way to publish an attorney's opinion and demonstrate her depth of knowledge on a particular topic. In this way, the attorney is positioned as a thought leader in her area of expertise. For further information on this useful tool, please refer to Chapter 4.

The Letter to the Editor

Another great way to reach out to the media and to have your voice heard is to write a letter to the editor (also known as commentary).

Writing a letter to the editor is a useful opportunity to share your opinion, educate the public about your issues, applaud someone for doing the right thing, or criticize policies that you believe should be changed. A well-written, well-timed letter to the editor can shift public opinion and influence policy as well as garner substantial media attention.

Think about it this way: How many times have you read a newspaper story that left you feeling bewildered, uninformed or disheartened? Think hard. I'm sure you can answer, "Often." You likely look at several newspapers every day. There are always stories that touch on subjects that are near and dear to your heart and practice. Whether it's a story about medical malpractice caps in your state, a study that reveals the prevalence of racial disparity in nursing home care or an article about the Fed's monetary and fiscal policies—there is always something to which you can respond. When you hear yourself say, "That's bull. This person has no idea what he's talking about," "This article doesn't even mention...," or "This should have at least addressed," then it's time to write your letter. Here's how:

Preparation

First and foremost, review the paper's policies and guidelines for submitting letters. Many have word count limitations and submission requirements that you absolutely must follow. Second, editors prefer to publish timely, concise letters that respond to an article, editorial or other letter that appeared in the newspaper and are relevant to issues of local or regional importance. When I say timely, I mean within 24 hours of the original article if you're writing to a daily publication. If you're responding to a weekly, give yourself no more than 48 hours, depending on its print cycle.

What to say

Your letter must be able to stand on its own. Remember, not all readers will have seen the original article. Therefore, open your letter with a strong statement that comments on the original article. Your opening comments can take issue with a statement made by the journalist, agree with and support an important point, clarify a comment made by someone who was interviewed for the original story, add discussion points about something readers would need to know, disagree with an editorial position, introduce a little-known fact or issue related to the subject, or point out an error or misrepresentation in the article. Be careful about accuracy and avoid personal attacks. Your letter must remain short and focused. Close with the thought you most want readers to remember. Think of your opening and closing statements at a trial. The concept is the same—it's just the number of words that have to be truncated.

Remember the details

Be sure to include your full name, the firm for which you work, your address, office phone number, cell phone number and e-mail address. Editors are wary of fake letters or those written just to promote a product or company, so most will contact you to verify that you wrote your letter and that you are providing the paper with permission to publish it. Finally, ask a colleague to review your letter to be sure your writing is clear, that you are getting your point across, and that there are no grammatical or spelling errors.

How to submit

Submit letters by e-mail whenever possible. Look for the e-mail address on the publication's Web site. If you can't find the editor's e-mail address, then use the outlet's Web site submission form to send your letter. If all else fails, send a fax. If you're writing to a small local weekly in your hometown, just send the letter via snail mail.

Here are some additional tips to keep in mind when submitting a letter to the editor:

• Avoid using legal jargon.

• Write from your heart. Be passionate.

• Don't respond to numerous articles in a short amount of time. Pick your battles wisely.

• Where possible, use facts, statistics, citations or other evidence to help illustrate your point.

• Anticipate that your letter will be shortened. Make sure you lead with your most important points and include a strong message in each paragraph.

• Use examples that relate to local readers. Editors are more likely to print letters with a local angle.

• Do not include a litany of self-serving commentary and details of your years of experience.

Letters to the editor are one of the most frequently read sections of the newspaper and are always published in the editorial section. When done right, your inclusion in this popular venue will accord you a great deal of credibility and recognition from those you wish to influence.

The Q and A

Questions and answers can be used in a myriad of ways in your public relations efforts. One way is to draft frequently asked questions and their answers to provide to members of the media. These can also be used to optimize your Web site. Another way is to prepare you and other members of your firm for questions the media might ask.

I counsel all my clients to keep a notebook next to the business phone they use most frequently. Every question they are asked that pertains to their general practices, business procedures or strategies should be recorded in the notebook.

For example, I am always asked, "How much will public relations cost our firm?" I then have to explain that public relations must be a strategic part of a firm's communications efforts. I say, "We cannot provide you with a budget until we've determined your goals and objectives, target audiences, and so on." Now, when a reporter interviewing me about communications strategies for law firms asks me that same question, I have my answer organized and available.

This same tactic works for communicating the allegations of a complaint, the responses to a defendant's answer, the alleged facts of a case or the outcome of a matter. While you're going through the trial, you should keep a separate list of Q&As. These questions are often the same as the questions you want to answer for a judge or jury. Then draft your answers carefully. You can then provide your Q&A documents to members of the media with whom you are corresponding. It helps to control the message and keep you on point.

The Fact Sheet

The fact sheet is very similar to a backgrounder. It provides background information but, more specifically, it provides facts that support the news you are sharing with the media. The fact sheet must be short and concise.

Think of it this way. If you have settled a very detailed case and you are sharing the news of the settlement with the media via a press release, you may want to include general noncontroversial facts about the case in a one- to two-page fact sheet.

Though fact sheets can stand alone, they are more commonly submitted along with a press release or media kit. You should include the basic who, what, when, where, why and how. Don't forget to include a contact name and information and a subject line or title.

SAMPLE FACT SHEET

Returning to the sample firm Buck & Fawn, take a look at a fact sheet detailing an event at which new partner Jane Doe will be a featured speaker. Jane is slated to address medical malpractice defense issues at her state's health care summit. Her firm would like the media to cover Pennsylvania's Medical Malpractice issues in favor of medical and insurance providers.

FACT SHEET

Buck & Fawn P.C. Attorneys at Law

Contact: Judy Smith, Communications Director
215.555.0212 or judysmith@buckfawnlaw.com

June 10, 2009

The Pennsylvania Medical Malpractice "Crisis"

Jane Doe, Esq., Partner, Buck & Fawn P.C.
Gov. Edwin D. Roobell will meet with state officials and industry leaders to examine the current availability and cost of medical malpractice liability insurance for physicians in Pennsylvania. Jane Doe, Esq., will provide a defense attorney's perspective on these issues.

When: August 10, 2009, at 10 a.m.

Where: Harrisburg Government Building, 11 North 3rd Street, Harrisburg, Pa.

Information: This program is free, but all attendees are required to register in advance by July 5, 2009. To register, call Judy Smith at 215.555.0212 or go to www.buckfawnlaw.com/register81009.

FACTS:

- Physicians are leaving Pennsylvania at an alarming rate.

- Malpractice insurance costs for physicians are rising.

- A recent study indicates that only 4.7 percent of doctors are responsible for 51.4 percent for all malpractice payments, according to a report from Public Citizen.

- A U.S. Department of Health and Human Services (HHS) report says that the malpractice crisis is threatening access to care.

- Doctors spend 3.2 percent of their income on malpractice costs.

- Pennsylvania physicians, particularly specialists, pay up to 5 times more for malpractice coverage than their colleagues in neighboring states.

- Physicians in eastern Pennsylvania have seen their annual malpractice premiums more than double, in some cases to over $100,000 per doctor.

Buck & Fawn P.C. is a national law firm of more than 1,000 lawyers specializing in civil defense litigation. Founded in 1920, Buck & Fawn is headquartered in Philadelphia, Pa., and maintains additional offices in Akron, Ohio; New York, N.Y.; Wilmington, Del.; and Los Angeles, Calif. Buck & Fawn has successfully defended clients ranging from Fortune 500 companies to local sole proprietors. Capabilities include insurance defense, employment matters, contract disputes and SEC litigation. For additional information, please see Buck & Fawn's Web site, www.buckfawnlaw.com.

The Calendar Listing

A calendar listing is a communiqué that is used to get a free listing of an event or program mentioned by media outlets that provide upcoming event information to their audiences. Calendar listings are issued in advance of an event and are intended to increase awareness and attendance of the program. If your event is by invitation only, a calendar listing should NOT be issued.

It is very important to find out when and to whom your listings should be sent. There is usually a calendar or events editor assigned to this information for print publications. Television and radio stations usually accept calendar listings for and via their Web sites.

The length of time in advance of the event is determined by the frequency of the medium and their editorial management preferences.

If you want the calendar listing in a monthly print publication, you may need to provide it with the calendar listing at least 60 days in advance. Weeklies often require two to three weeks, and dailies usually require at least one week's notice. Also be aware that many Web sites provide you with the ability to upload the information yourself and, once approved (usually within 24 hours), will post it online.

SAMPLE CALENDAR LISTING

Take a look at a calendar listing detailing an event using Jane Doe's speaking engagement. Jane is slated to address medical malpractice defense issues at her state's health care summit. Her firm would like insurance companies, medical providers and in-house counsel from health care institutions to know about this speaking engagement.

CALENDAR LISTING

Buck & Fawn P.C. Attorneys at Law

> **Contact:** Judy Smith, Communications Director
> 215.555.0212 or judysmith@buckfawnlaw.com

June 10, 2009

Jane Doe, Esq., to Provide Insight into Pennsylvania Medical Malpractice "Crisis" at Pennsylvania Health Care Summit

Insurance Defense Lawyer Will Address the Current State of Malpractice Liability Insurance in Pennsylvania for Insurance Companies, Medical Providers and Health Care Institutions

Who: Jane Doe, Esq., Partner, Buck & Fawn P.C. will join Gov. Edwin D. Roobell, state officials and industry leaders to examine the current availability and cost of medical malpractice liability insurance for physicians in Pennsylvania. Jane Doe, Esq., will provide a defense attorney's perspective on these issues.

When: August 10, 2009, at 10 a.m.

Where: Harrisburg Government Building, 11 North 3rd Street, Harrisburg, Pa.

Information: This program is free, but all attendees are required to register in advance by July 5, 2009. To register, call Judy Smith at 215.555.0212 or go to www.buckfawnlaw.com/register81009.

Why: Pennsylvania's medical malpractice insurance industry has been in a state of flux for the past decade. As headlines warn that physicians are leaving the state due to the increasing cost of malpractice insurance, opponents of tort reform contend that the situation is not as dire as it appears. Recently, a major charitable organization completed an in-depth study into the state of malpractice liability insurance in Pennsylvania. Government officials and industry leaders are now poised to examine the results of this research endeavor and chart a path designed to benefit health care consumers and physicians.

About Jane Doe, Esq.: Jane Doe, Esq., has been representing insurance providers and insureds for more than two decades. She recently joined leading defense firm Buck & Fawn P.C. as a partner in the Insurance Defense Litigation Group. Notably, Doe successfully represented a major hospital in a $5 million medical malpractice matter.

Buck & Fawn P.C. is a national law firm of more than 1,000 lawyers specializing in civil defense litigation. Founded in 1920, Buck & Fawn is headquartered in Philadelphia, Pa., and maintains additional offices in Akron, Ohio; New York, N.Y.; Wilmington, Del.; and Los Angeles, Calif. Buck & Fawn has successfully defended clients ranging from Fortune 500 companies to local sole proprietors. Capabilities include insurance defense, employment matters, contract disputes and SEC litigation. For additional information, please see Buck & Fawn's Web site, www.buckfawnlaw.com.

The Media Advisory

A media advisory is most often used to entice members of the press to attend an upcoming event. Much shorter than a press release, a media advisory still covers who, what, when, where and why, but it does so without "giving away the farm." Unlike a press release, a media advisory is not meant to be a pseudo news story. Rather, it should be a succinctly written enticement similar to a save-the-date notice, which alerts reporters and editors to a future event or story opportunity. Media advisories might, for example, be sent out in advance of a press conference, to announce that a major class action complaint has been filed, before an important speaking engagement, to unveil new offices or for a groundbreaking ceremony.

Because your advisory is meant to persuade reporters to attend your event, it should not provide so much information that a reporter could write her story without actually showing up. Accordingly, keep the advisory to one page and do not include too much detailed information. It is common practice to lead with a tantalizing headline (and possibly a subhead) and then to follow with the who, what, when, where and why. After a short paragraph explaining the "why," you might also wish to include a brief background paragraph. You should conclude your advisory with the same boilerplate you would place at the end of a press release.

SAMPLE MEDIA ADVISORY

This time, Buck & Fawn's goal is to get members of the media to attend the program in Harrisburg, Pa., so take a look at a media advisory detailing the event at which Jane Doe will be a featured speaker:

MEDIA ADVISORY

Buck & Fawn P.C. Attorneys at Law

Contact: Judy Smith, Communications Director
215.555.0212 or judysmith@buckfawnlaw.com

June 10, 2009

Jane Doe, Esq., to Provide Insight into Pennsylvania Medical Malpractice "Crisis" at Pennsylvania Health Care Summit
Insurance Defense Lawyer Will Address State Officials and Industry Leaders as They Examine the Current State of Malpractice Liability Insurance in Pennsylvania

Who: Jane Doe, Esq., Partner, Buck & Fawn P.C.

What: Gov. Edwin D. Roobell will meet with state officials and industry leaders to examine the current availability and cost of medical malpractice liability insurance for physicians in Pennsylvania. Jane Doe, Esq., will provide a defense attorney's perspective on these issues.

When: August 10, 2009, at 10 a.m.

Where: Harrisburg Government Building, 11 North 3rd Street, Harrisburg, Pa.

Why: Pennsylvania's medical malpractice insurance industry has been in a state of flux for the past decade. As headlines warn that physicians are leaving the state due to the increasing cost of malpractice insurance, opponents of tort reform contend that the situation is not as dire as it appears. Recently, a major charitable organization completed an in-depth study into the state of malpractice liability insurance in Pennsylvania. Government officials and industry leaders are now poised to examine the results of this research endeavor and chart a path designed to benefit health care consumers and physicians.

About Jane Doe, Esq.: Jane Doe, Esq., has been representing insurance providers and insureds for more than two decades. She recently joined leading defense firm Buck & Fawn P.C. as a partner in the Insurance Defense Litigation Group. Notably, Doe successfully represented a major hospital in a $5 million medical malpractice matter.

Buck & Fawn P.C. is a national law firm of more than 1,000 lawyers specializing in civil defense litigation. Founded in 1920, Buck & Fawn is headquartered in Philadelphia, Pa., and maintains additional offices in Akron, Ohio; New York, N.Y.; Wilmington, Del.; and Los Angeles, Calif. Buck & Fawn has successfully defended clients ranging from Fortune 500 companies to local sole proprietors. Capabilities include insurance defense, employment matters, contract disputes and SEC litigation. For additional information, please see Buck & Fawn's Web site, www.buckfawnlaw.com.

Here are some additional tips to help you issue successful media advisories:

- Send your advisory out approximately four weeks in advance of the event so reporters can make arrangements to attend.

- Resend the advisory the day before the event.

- If there will be a photo opportunity, live video feed or other visual opportunities, include that information in your advisory.

- Keep the advisory to one page.

- Issue your advisory on firm letterhead if sending by mail.

- Mail the advisory in a colored envelope labeled "Invitation to VIPs."

- Issue your advisory in the body of the e-mail, not as an attachment, if you plan to send it electronically.

- As with a press release, remember to conduct research to ensure that the advisory is sent to the appropriate editors and reporters the way they wish to be contacted.

- If necessary, include directions and information about parking, refreshments and accommodations.

- Follow up with a phone call as the event date approaches.

Remember that a media advisory should be punchy and enticing. You want to convince the press to attend your event or cover your story, so keep the piece short; but be sure to let them know why your item is worthy of attention.

The Press Kit

A press kit, also known as a media kit, is a vital tool in public relations. It is a collection of information about your organization, your news story, the players, the issues and the experts who can discuss the matters that affect you and your target audiences. It should be used as a way to provide more details to the media, not as a primary tool to pitch to the media.

Press kits are especially vital in working with journalists. They save time and improve accuracy by providing the basic information that journalists need for their reports.

What to include in your press kit (hard copy and on a CD-ROM):
- Biographies of individuals who play key roles in the firm or in relation to the story or issue you are addressing
- Firm backgrounder
- Mission statement
- Q&As
- Fact sheets
- Recent press releases

- Photos (in 5 x 7 or 8 x 10 hard copy and on a CD-ROM)
- Copies of relevant news clippings and reprints

Here are some additional tips to keep in mind:

Include a cover letter: The cover letter should indicate what is included in the kit and who to contact for additional information. Insert a business card into the slits of a pocket folder or attach it to your cover letter.

Press kits won't help you if you don't pass them out: Keep press kits on hand at the office, at trade shows, at community events you attend and at any company events. Make your press kits readily available to every news outlet you encounter. Make a note on your Web site that press kits are always available to members of the media. Provide an e-mail link for media requests and make the kit available as a downloadable file.

Encourage members of the press to contact you: Place a Rolodex card in your press kit. Often reporters will toss the press kit but hold onto the Rolodex card. Make sure to include as much information as you can on the card. You can also include a mini-CD with your v-card and other pertinent information.

Look the part: Use firm letterhead for each element of the press kit. This looks professional and ensures that your contact information is always at hand.

Keep it current: Update your press kit frequently by including current press releases and news coverage. Publications always want the latest, most up-to-date information about your firm.

The Press Conference

Ah, the infamous press conference. Without fail, attorneys ask me to "call a press conference" every time they perceive their case or story to be important. The truth is that every case is important to the attorney and to her clients; however, the same is not the case when talking about the media and consumer audiences. It's like trying to sell the house that you have built. Most buyers won't care if you purchased all new designer furniture, not unless you are planning to include it in the purchase price of the house.

A press conference involves someone speaking to the media at a predetermined time and place. The speaker controls the information she delivers and the media she invites to hear that information. There is also a presumption that the speaker will answer questions posed by the media or other attendees.

When to call a press conference

So, then, when does it make sense to call a press conference? Ask yourself: Is this the type of story that the media will eat up? Does it involve death, scandal, consumer fraud, corporate misconduct or criminal activities? Have your target media outlets covered similar topics in the past? Does your story have wide appeal?

The bottom line: Ask yourself who cares about the topic. Not every trial result makes sense for a press conference.

As a rule of thumb, the only time a press conference makes sense is if your story warrants television coverage. Otherwise, it's easier and less expensive to contact individual members of the media with your story.

Preparing for your press conference

As with any event, you need to go through a strategic planning process. A press conference is no different. It must be well planned and strategically executed in order to be successful. In fact, it's not just who you invite but when you invite them that makes a large difference.

For example, if you want to get coverage on the evening news, you should plan your press conference between 10 a.m. and 11 a.m. That will give the reporters and camera crews enough time to attend your program, script their voiceovers, edit the film and have it on the production floor in time for the evening news. It is rare that your press conference will be covered live unless it's a matter that is taking place on the courthouse steps on a case that has high publicity appeal.

If you are going to host the press conference at your office, town hall or other similar venue, you need to determine the logistics of space and time. Consider seating, parking and refreshments. If the press conference is in your office, you also need to make sure other clients' files are secured and not in plain view of your attendees.

Also think about the backdrop behind the speaker. This is extremely important because, if there are any wide-angle views, everything comes into play. Is your firm name and logo apparent? Are there any distractions? If you are at the site of an incident or at a corporate location, is there a view that tells the story?

During the spring of 2007, the law firm of Saltz Mongeluzzi Barrett & Bendesky P.C. of Philadelphia reached a global settlement worth more than $101 million. The settlement stemmed from the October 2003 collapse of the Tropicana Casino parking garage in Atlantic City, N.J. Thirty-six people were injured, four of whom died. Bob Mongeluzzi, Esq., was the primary plaintiffs' spokesperson at the press conference regarding the settlement, which was touted as "the largest verdict in a construction accident in American history."

The press conference was held live at the scene of the accident, where Mogeluzzi said, "While the wounds occurred on October 30, 2003, the scars will never heal. This is a shocking...outrageous oversight, and it cost four men their lives." Paul D'Amato, Esq., plaintiffs' co-counsel from New Jersey, said, "And let us hope that this is the last casino project that will be rushed on the broken bones of construction workers."

Not only did plaintiffs' counsel choose the right location, but their words were perfect sound bites that caught the attention of news viewers everywhere. The press conference was well planned and executed. It is obvious that plaintiffs' counsel in this matter were well prepared for their press conference.

PRESS CONFERENCE CHECKLIST

_____ Targeted media invitation list
_____ Location, date, time and duration
_____ Media advisory and directions
_____ List of speakers with printed biographies
_____ Press kits
_____ Prepared Q&A for speakers
_____ Media training for speakers
_____ Refreshments and rental needs/seating for media
_____ Sound system and podium or lectern (conduct a sound check)
_____ Banner/backdrop with firm name and logo for photos
_____ Parking
_____ Follow-up

As with all public relations efforts, it is important to identify what you want to accomplish first. Once you know your goal, you can then pick and choose among the media outreach tools that will accomplish your objectives. They're not all meant to be used in a vacuum, and not every tool is right for every message. Think strategically, just as you would when choosing which evidence to present to the jury.

CHAPTER NINE

> Nobody counts the number of ads you run;
> they just remember the impression you make.
> —*William Bernbach*

Leveraging Everyday Tools to Leave a Lasting Impression

I often speak at bar association conferences on public relations for lawyers, and usually I open with the following questions: "How many of you use e-mail as a communications tool in your practice?" "How many of you have voicemail in your office and on your cell phones?" "How many of you attend social and business functions on a regular basis?" Then I ask, "How many of you have someone else's voice on your voicemail message?" I immediately say, "Please don't answer that—the question is rhetorical."

There are countless encounters with our target audiences on a daily basis. We have the power to control the messages that we use in order to leverage everyday tools to leave a lasting impression.

Your 30-Second Introduction

Some say you need them. Others say you don't. I can tell you that I loathe the "30-second commercial," but I know that it's important to be able to articulate who I am and what I do quickly and effectively. Your 30-second commercial or introduction is a critical tool that needs to be carefully tailored so you don't sound silly.

I once attended a seminar by Michael Port, author of *Book Yourself Solid*. Michael asked the attendees, "How many of you enjoy introducing yourselves with a 30-second commercial?" No one raised her hand. So why would I start this chapter with the 30-second commercial? Because, with the competition so fierce today, associates and partners alike know they have to network and market themselves—which means introducing oneself over and over again. Yet when I ask someone at a Bar function, "What do you do?" the answer is usually, "I'm an attorney." My silent response? "No kidding!"

What a wasted opportunity! It is up to you to communicate what you do, and you need to do it quickly and effectively. That usually means in 30 seconds or less. A 30-second commercial (a.k.a. the elevator pitch) is a short, concise, compelling and creative summary of who you are and what you do. It is used when you meet people for the first time and they ask about your business. It is used as your outgoing voicemail message. It is used by others who refer business to you, in your prospective client meetings, at your dinner table and just about anywhere you discuss your business. It is not meant to sound like a television commercial.

Imagine this: "Hello. I'm Fawn Spring. I am a medical malpractice attorney. I represent people in Alabama who have been seriously hurt by doctors or hospitals. What's important to me is that I help my clients find the resources they need to move on in their lives and become a little bit more whole. I have an 800 number where I can be reached. It is 800-DOCLAWS, and my Web site is similar; it is www.doclaws.com."

One of the most challenging things to do for most attorneys, however, is to produce a solid 30-second introduction. Every professional should have something effective to say that has been prepared and rehearsed, and is ready when you are networking, contacting the media or talking to a prospective client or employer. Call it a "30-second commercial," an "elevator speech" or a "pitch." Just know that you have a very short time to get your message across.

So what should you say? Start with the introduction. Be brief but memorable. Tell who you are, what you do, who you serve and how your work benefits others. Make it easy to understand and compelling enough to leave the listener wanting to know more. For example:

> "I'm Mark Geragos, a criminal defense attorney. I represent and defend the rights of the well-known and the well-heeled in the glare of national media attention."
>
> **Or**
>
> "I'm Mark Geragos. I serve as counsel for very famous and often unsympathetic defendants, such as Michael Jackson and Scott Peterson, who were involved in major scandals. I work to get a fair trial despite public pressure."

You need to state the benefits of working with you, crisply and concisely. Revisit the Mark Geragos examples. The benefits: "represent and defend the rights" or "serve as counsel for very famous and often unsympathetic defendants."

What does this brief introduction do for you? It tells the listener about your specific, unique and impressive attributes. It allows you to appear more poised and confident. If done well, your introduction should invite more detailed and qualifying questions.

Again, look at Mark Geragos's introduction, "I represent and defend the rights of the well-known and the well-heeled in the glare of national media attention." This introduction begs the question, "So who have you represented?" Or "I work to get a fair trial despite public pressure." This makes your listeners ask you to explain how you've done that.

Now you can have a more detailed and memorable conversation.

EVERYDAY PUBLIC RELATIONS FOR LAWYERS

That may be fine for a narrowly focused attorney like Mark Geragos, you say, but how should general practice and multipractice attorneys introduce themselves when they have so much to say? Keep it simple. Know your audiences and prepare different introductions for each encounter.

For example, Mary Smith is a plaintiffs' attorney with a general practice. She attends a criminal law CLE. She can introduce either her general practice or a niche practice:

> "Hi, I'm Mary Smith. I am a Miami plaintiffs' attorney—I handle automobile accidents, medical malpractice, wills and estates, workers' compensation, social security disability and real estate matters."
> **Or**
> "Hi, I'm Mary Smith, a Miami medical malpractice plaintiff's attorney. I help clients understand when they have a case and why it is okay to sue doctors if they've made a mistake."

The second example is much more memorable. If this is a continuing legal education class, the audience already knows that plaintiffs' attorneys practice in other areas of the law.

That's why you need to consider the audience and create different introductions for different purposes and venues. Your introduction to prospective referring attorneys will differ from your introduction to prospective clients.

To start, ask yourself the following questions:
- Where am I going (venue)?
- Who is going to be there (target audience)?
- What do I want to accomplish/get across to those in attendance (key messages)?
- What are the benefits of working with me?
- Why should listeners care? (What is in it for them?)

Plan your introduction well before your meeting. Focus on one specific practice area or niche. Then write it down, rehearse it and time yourself.

The following tips will help you prepare your 30-second introduction.

DO:

- Remember that every word counts
- Be specific
- Engage the listener, grab her attention, and get her interested in the conversation
- Think in terms of benefits to your listeners (what's in it for them)
- Concentrate on what the listener wants and needs to hear
- Tailor your words to the listener's needs
- Keep in mind your tone of voice
- Be enthusiastic
- Invest time on a regular basis to revise your pitch
- Keep your commercial current and original
- Incorporate your tagline if appropriate
- Remember to deliver contact information
- Keep it short —7 to 30 seconds
- Follow up

On the other hand, DON'T:

- Talk all about you
- Summarize your job description and call that your commercial
- Use general language or jargon
- Sound like a salesman
- Speak in a monotone voice
- Memorize your pitch word for word
- Cross your arms and look down at the floor while speaking
- Compare your company to your perceived competition
- Appear rehearsed

Anything more than 30 seconds will be lost in translation and deflected by distraction. You have 30 seconds—make the most of it!

Your Voicemail Messages Make Lasting Impressions

In today's day and age, we spend more time leaving messages and listening to recordings than we do interacting one-on-one with our public. So it is that much more important to have a great voicemail message.

When was the last time you listened to your outgoing office voicemail message? Is it recorded in your voice? What about your cell phone message? Don't say that you recorded it on a speaker while driving from your home to court during rush hour.

Every time someone calls you and hears your voicemail message, they should be happy to leave a message. It is often the first time someone "interacts" with you. Make it friendly, energetic, informative and compelling.

Stand up when you record your voicemail into your handheld device. Do not use speakerphone. Don't forget to say your company name and what it is you do. If you have a home-based office, shut off the television and the radio. Go into a closed room where there will be no distractions from significant others, children or pets. Write down what you plan to say, then stand up and record it on your outgoing voicemail message. Use your best voice, too. Remember that speaking to a caller is no different than speaking to the jury. In both cases, you're being judged.

If you're trying to get a television or radio interview, you should also know that some producers will call off-hours to get a feel for your voice and how you speak. If you sound awful, the likelihood is that the listener is going to get a bad first impression.

Your E-Mail Signature: Not an Afterthought

Some attorneys have them and some don't. Some attorneys are still using AOL and Yahoo! to communicate with their public. If this is you, read on. You need to use your e-mail signature to say more.

An e-mail signature is a block of text attached to an e-mail message that typically contains contact information, such as your name, title, company name, phone, fax, mobile, e-mail and Web site address. Some people prefer to just include their names and addresses in their signatures, while others like to share a quote with the e-mail recipient.

Make sure that you separate your signature from the body of your message. Limit it to four to seven lines and be creative. Do not include images. One example of an effective signature would be to include a link to your firm's Web site, which can result in increased Web traffic.

Use your e-mail signature to your advantage. Restate your company mission, add a favorite quote or place a link to a news article about you or your company. If you are going to be presenting at an open-forum conference, let the recipient know. It's the easiest and least-expensive way to reinforce what's going on with your company and your clients without being obnoxious and intrusive. Whatever you do, make sure your contact information is included.

Your Google Maps Listing

Google and other major search engines such as Yahoo!, MSN, AOL and ask.com (formerly AskJeeves) are now front doors to your business. Since Google launched GoogleMaps (maps.google.com), it is imperative that you register your firm's address or addresses. Go to the Local Business Center of Google Maps on the Internet. Create a free account with Google and then follow the user-friendly steps to register your company. This will allow you to come up in the map listings when someone searches for your services in your region.

Industry Associations: Not Just for Your Resume

Active participation in industry associations builds credibility and name recognition in your industry and target industries. It is important for your peers to identify you as an expert for referrals. But just like sponsorships, if you're not present, it doesn't really matter if you pay annual dues. There are plenty of organizations across the country. Take advantage of them and the networking opportunities they offer.

Now let's jump to the next chapter to further investigate using the Web to reach your target audiences. Though some attorneys still have their assistants manage and type their e-mails, none of us can ignore the power of the Internet. The Web is increasingly becoming the first place that people look for virtually all kinds of information. You, too, can harness its power to attract and retain business.

CHAPTER TEN

> Once we rid ourselves of traditional thinking,
> we can get on with creating the future.
> —*James Bertrand*

The New World
of Communication

There are many days that I declare traditional media gone forever. I know it's not true (yet), but the ways in which we deliver and receive information are rapidly changing. Initially, the only ways to reach one's audience were through print and radio. Using these media, it was very difficult to influence a wide audience quickly. With the advent of television, however, suddenly one could reach 50 million people, but it took 13 years. This is approximately one-third of the time that it took using radio advertising to reach the same number of listeners.

Now, with the proliferation of the Internet, the time it takes to reach 50 million people has decreased, in most cases, to four years. That's great news for those who need to promote their businesses. But Web 2.0 is not for the faint of heart. The new world of communication requires stalwart, tenacious and persistent attention, along with the ability to adapt to rapid change.

EVERYDAY PUBLIC RELATIONS FOR LAWYERS

It's Not Your Father's Mainframe Anymore

Remember when having a home computer was a novelty? When the machines were cumbersome, the printing achingly slow and the discs fragile? Well, times they are a-changin'.

In March 2006, the Pew Charitable Trusts completed its Internet & American Life Project study, which revealed that "some 50 million Americans turn to the Internet for news on a typical day." This is not a surprise, as Americans have increasingly turned to high-speed broadband Internet connections, researchers concluded. In fact, between 2002 and 2006, Internet use rose from 58 percent of all adult Americans to 70 percent, they found. Meanwhile, home broadband penetration grew from 20 million people (10 percent of adult Americans) to 74 million people (37 percent of adult Americans). These numbers continue to grow exponentially each year. As of July 2006, 71 percent of all adult Americans were using the Internet.

Forget the days of the simple answering machine, radio or beeper. Amazingly, the Consumer Electronics Association of America in 2007 learned that the average American home now has 26 different electronic devices for communication and media.

If you can believe it, in 2007 the Association was tracking sales and consumer preferences for 53 separate gadgets. Who knows how many gadgets will be available just a few years after this book is first published. Heck, look at Apple's iPhone, released in June 2007 and marketed as a mobile phone revolution. This new phone, which sold for approximately $400, was a multimedia device that could be used for taking pictures, playing music and videos, watching television, surfing the Internet and sending and receiving e-mail, among other functions. There is no doubt that putting so many functions into portable devices like the iPhone has changed the way we work and communicate.

Bearing this out, a May 2007 Pew Charitable Trusts study entitled "A Typology of Information and Communication Technology Users" revealed that:

- 8 percent of Americans are deep users of the participatory Web and mobile applications;

- 23 percent are heavy, pragmatic tech adopters—they use gadgets to keep up with social networks or be more productive at work;

- 10 percent rely on mobile devices for voice, texting or entertainment;

- 10 percent use information gadgets but find it a hassle;

- 49 percent of Americans only occasionally use modern gadgetry, and many others bristle at electronic connectivity.

In fact, the number of text messages sent and received today via electronic devices exceeds the population of the planet.

Clearly, this abundance of options affects the way American consumers spend their time, gather information, and make decisions about the products and services they would like to purchase. No wonder a study from Ball State University revealed that on a typical day, the average American spends more time using media devices—television, radio, iPods and cell phones—than any other activity while awake. About 30 percent of the observed waking day was spent with media as the sole activity, compared to 21 percent spent on work activity, with an additional 39 percent devoted to media in conjunction with some other activity. Let's not forget that many—if not most—of these devices are wireless and therefore mobile.

TODAY'S 21-YEAR-OLDS HAVE . . .

- Watched 20,000 hours of television;
- Played 10,000 hours of video games;
- Talked 10,000 hours on the telephone;
- Sent and received 250,000 e-mails or instant messages.

In addition, 50 percent of them have created content on the Web.

And to think many of us did not even touch a computer before we entered college or the workforce!

But understanding and embracing these statistics is only the first step. The next step is to learn the various ways to communicate via the Internet and to capitalize on these technologies to reach your target audiences, especially our future decision makers, who undoubtedly communicate much differently than we did just 10 years ago.

So, how can lawyers grow their businesses online? Simple (well, not really): as with other forms of public relations, taking advantage of the World Wide Web requires an integrated and strategic approach. The first step is to remember what you learned in Chapter 1: You have to understand who you're trying to influence and why. Once you know who you want to reach, then it's imperative to research where these audiences are online. Since we've already established that 71 percent of the American adult buying audience is wired, let's talk about the various ways to reach them.

From Britannica to Wikipedia, Web 2.0 at Its Best

Web 2.0, a term said to be coined by Tim O'Reilly, refers to a perceived second generation of Web-based communities and hosted services—such as blogging, social media, wikis and other online tools that facilitate collaboration and sharing between users. O'Reilly Media titled a series of conferences around the phrase, and it has since become widely adopted.

Although the term suggests a new version of the World Wide Web, it does not refer to an update to the Web's technical specifications but rather to changes in the ways we use the Internet. According to O'Reilly, "Web 2.0 is the business revolution in the computer industry caused by the move to the Internet as platform and an attempt to understand the rules for success on that new platform."

Originally, the World Wide Web was considered just another medium to communicate traditional information. You could read the same news articles that were in print publications, you could see the same branded, one-dimensional ads that were available in print forms, Web sites were all glorified brochures (which communication industry folks coined "brochureware"), and television and radio stations were just promoting their lineup and schedules online.

But then, with the new millennium, the entire landscape changed. Television programs such as news and reality shows began driving traffic to their Web sites. News anchors started blogging. Commercials could be skipped with Tivo and other DVRs. And people began networking online instead of meeting in public.

Friending for Life: We're Not in Kansas Anymore

The advances in how we use the Web didn't stop with business applications; perhaps the most obvious and headline-grabbing changes took place with the launch of sites like MySpace, Facebook, Bebo, Orkut, Hi5, Friendster, Match, Eons and other "social networking" Web sites, which have attracted children, teens and adults alike in astounding numbers. In fact, reports indicated that by 2007, more than 100 million people worldwide were logging onto these virtual meeting places. What are they? Essentially, they are online communities (there are hundreds of them) that permit members to share personal information and meet others with similar interests so they can become "friends." They are usually free to join. Users can search for other members and contact them by leaving comments on their profile pages or through e-mail, instant messaging, chat rooms or discussion boards. Toto, I don't think we're in Kansas anymore.

SOCIAL MEDIA STATS MID-2007

According to a global social networking study released in July 2007 by comScore (NASDAQ: SCOR), a leader in measuring the digital world, social networking behemoth MySpace attracted more than 114 million global visitors aged 15 years and older. This represented a 72 percent increase in use from June 2006 to June 2007. Similarly, Facebook jumped 270 percent to 52.2 million visitors. Bebo increased 172 percent to 18.2 million visitors, and Tagged went up 774 percent to 13.2 million visitors.

So, how does one harness social networking in everyday public relations?

Think about the word "relations." That's exactly what social networking sites create in the most basic sense of the term: a relationship between one person and another, where the two have agreed to be associated. By joining a social network and talking about the things that are important to you, you will ultimately make friends (I use the term loosely) with people who have similar interests.

Keep in mind, however, that even your social networking page or pages will be scrutinized by your peers and hence may be subject to the rules of professional conduct in your state and others. If you're going to use these tools, be radically transparent. Let people know you're an attorney, that you're not there to solicit business or give legal advice, and, somewhere on the page, be sure to add comprehensive disclaimers. It's likely only a matter of time until an overzealous tribunal determines that all online communications are considered legal communications.

As far as the effectiveness of social networking, some legal marketers believe it is a great tool for creating relationships that will turn into business. Others oppose the thought. I'm still on the fence because I haven't seen the proof in the pudding.

So, up until a few weeks before this book went to print, I didn't have a profile on MySpace or Facebook. Why? Because I wasn't sure I wanted to spend my time keeping them fresh and up-to-date. My view on this is quickly changing, though, as I continue to harness the powers of these online tools. It now seems imperative to have a presence on these and other social networking sites.

But fear not: never have there been more low-cost or cost-free opportunities to promote ourselves and our businesses without leaving our offices. With mere keystrokes, we can update clients on firm news, announce big wins and welcome new hires. It's a whole new World Wide Web. If politicians are on board (when this book went to print, Hillary Clinton had nearly 150,000 friends on MySpace and nearly 52,000 friends on Facebook), you should be, too. Here's how.

Wikiing While You Work

A wiki is an open-forum Web site that allows people to collaborate and provide information on particular areas of interest. Most wikis can be accessed and edited by anyone.

THE NEW WORLD OF COMMUNICATION

When this book went to press, Wikipedia was the leading free encyclopedia, allowing "anyone [to] edit almost any page," according to the Wikipedia Web site. Therefore, as an attorney, you can add accurate information about changes to the law, legal trends and precedent-setting cases (especially those in which you had a role), and other factual information.

You also need to remember that anything you add can be edited by others. If you're going to provide content, be impartial and unbiased. Include all sides of the story.

Don't ever try to hide anything—if you do, you'll likely be called on the carpet. According to communication industry leaders Seth Godin and Chris Anderson, among others, the digital age of communication calls for *radical transparency*. If you try to hide something or just provide half-truths, you'll then need to read the "Crisis Communication Plan Components and Models" by The Lukaszewski Group.

Blogging for Apples

You've undoubtedly heard about "blogs" and "blogging," but, for the uninitiated, "blog" is short for "Web log." In the legal industry, they are also known as "blawgs," short for "law blogs." You can check out my blog at www.ThePR-Lawyer.com.

A Web log or law blog is a journal (or newsletter) that is frequently updated and intended for general public consumption. It is a way to encourage two-way conversation between the blog's author and contributors and those who wish to comment on the blog's contents. A blog generally represents the personality of the author, company or Web site that launched it.

Blogs are great tools for attorneys to establish themselves as leaders in their fields of practice and to establish an online social discourse. They should be used to have online discussions with target audiences, including prospective clients and the media. What's important to remember, though, is that your blog needs to be yours. It should reflect your voice and thoughts, not those of a marketing or public relations professional.

Kevin O'Keefe of LexBlog, the leading lawyer blog provider in the U.S., calls blogging "PR by participation." That means getting involved and engaging yourself in the online social conversation.

According to O'Keefe, "Blogs are imperative for attorneys who want to establish themselves in their areas of practice. However, they are not meant to be published by a PR agency or law firm communication folks. By their very nature, blogs are written by the lawyers participating in an online conversation on their niche area of expertise."

In 2007, Alan S. Rutkin, a partner in Rivkin Radler LLP of New York, launched the InsuranceCoverageLawyerBlog.com as part of his public relations plan to position him as a legal authority who focuses on the analysis, negotiation and litigation of disputes involving environmental matters, toxic torts and other complex claims. As a result of taking full advantage of Internet discussions, Mr. Rutkin is viewed as a reliable and trusted authority within his niche. Within two months of the blog's launch, InsuranceCoverageLawyerBlog.com was selected for the "Top Blogs" section of LexisNexis's Insurance Law Center.

Before you decide to blog, ask yourself a few critical questions:

- Does my firm have policies regarding blogs or other online discourse to which I am bound?

- Do I have a niche area of practice to which I currently or will in the future devote a substantial amount of my practice?

- Have I researched the market landscape and determined how I can create a competitive advantage?

- Is there an online audience who will care about what I have to say and be engaged by my commentary?

- Am I interested in providing valuable, meaningful content to my target audiences?

THE NEW WORLD OF COMMUNICATION

- Am I willing to set aside at least 15 minutes a day, at least three days per week?

- Do I have the time to commit long-term to manage a blog?

Once you've answered these questions, you will know whether blogging is right for you.

Blogging is also a great way to converse with members of the media. When you comment on media blogs or publish your own blog entries regarding the media and what they've said, you are creating a relationship and getting yourself on their radar screens. Many reporters today are also writing blogs. Their content may or may not be included in the print version of their newspaper or magazines, or on their television programs or radio shows. But it is, in fact, being included on the Web, and as Web 2.0 continues to grow, PR practitioners and media-savvy lawyers must add blog journalists to their lists of VIP media. Of course, adding them to your list is one thing; pitching them a story is another.

Steve Rubel (no relation to me, although we share the same last name and love of public relations), the author of Micropersuasion.com and a senior vice president in Edelman's me2revolution practice, has said that "Many in PR seem to be treating Web 2.0 as simply an extension of the traditional media—another venue for buzz. Online social networks and communities are completely different. Bloggers, social networkers, diggers, social bookmakers and Wikipedians don't want to be pitched. They're collaborating on these sites for a reason—to share, to be entertained, to become informed, to connect, etc. They place value on people who contribute regularly and selflessly."

In fact, it's against what's becoming known as blogger etiquette to send a press release to a blogger. They don't want your press releases. They want discourse and data: the two D's of blogger communications. They want discourse, which you will have to do via commenting on the original blog and/or adding blog entries to your own blog. They want data that matters to them. Tell them what's new in relation to what they already write about.

EVERYDAY PUBLIC RELATIONS FOR LAWYERS

Before reaching out to a blogger, answer some of these important blog relations questions:

- What can you contribute to this blog that the blogger hasn't already said?

- How can your information make a difference?

- Is your story or commentary relevant to this blog?
- Have you personalized your e-mail (you are using e-mail, right?) to meet the needs of the blogger?

- Does your e-mail make it easy for the blogger to copy and paste a few sentences, and I repeat, a FEW sentences, rather than a two-page press release?

BLOG RELATIONS WEB RESOURCES

- Andywibbels.com
- Badpitch.blogspot.com
- Businessblogconsulting.com
- Businessweek.com/the_thread/blogspotting
- Forward-moving.com
- Hyku.com
- Kevin.lexblog.com
- Mediabistro.com/mbtoolbox
- Micropersuasion.com

So the next step, once you're convinced that you need a blog as part of your public relations plan, is to figure out how you're going to create it. You have two choices: 1) create the blog yourself using one of the free sources on the Web, or 2) reach out to a professional to create the blog for you. There are many pros and cons to both approaches. If you decide to go it alone, the most well-known sources for creating free blogs include the Google-owned Blogger,

TypePad, Wordpress, and Movable Type (open source software). My advice, however, is that it's easier and more cost-effective in the long run to seek the professional services of a firm that specializes in creating blogs for lawyers.

After you've created your blog, and you're regularly populating it with great content, then make sure your blog can be found on sites such as Technorati, Bloghop, Icerocket, Blogdigger, Plazoo and Feedster.

Really Simple Syndication in the 21st Century

Really Simple Syndication or "RSS" is a technology that allows users to subscribe to news feeds, blogs, Web sites and other interactive online media to receive direct information to a "news aggregator." The news aggregator is similar to a mailbox or an e-mail inbox. It's a tool that Internet users can utilize to manage "RSS Feeds" in order to receive updates from the sources that they value most.

I often hear the phrase "push-pull technology." This means that if you are providing an RSS application with your Web site or blog, then you are "pushing" information to your target audiences. In the same vein, those people who are subscribing to your RSS feed are "pulling" the information they want to receive—that which they consider of value. Thus, it's a push-pull tool, unlike e-mail, which is a push-only technology.

There are many news aggregators, including Yahoo, Google, and NewsGator Online, which send updates to subscribers when their selected sites add new content or when a news story or blog post includes their chosen keywords. In this way, RSS and news aggregators can be used to distribute your latest information to your target audiences. Similarly, you can use these applications to stay current in your practice area or areas.

RSS has many additional public relations benefits. It can be used to track news about you, your firm and cases that you are handling. It can be used to monitor your competition. It can be used to stay on top of industry trends and research. It can be used to monitor your favorite reporters, publications, media outlets and editors to stay on top of their news preferences and styles.

RSS is just one of the many 21st-century technologies that appears to be working well for public relations practitioners. But, who knows, RSS could be outdated before 2010. The scary thing is that I still remember the first portable Mac®, when hard drives and modems were external and e-mail was for early adopters. Where has the time gone?

Ease on Down the E-zine

E-zine is short for "electronic magazine," though the term is also used to describe electronic newsletters. These electronic publications are typically sent out to subscribers who voluntarily sign up (opt in) to receive them.

The main purpose of an e-zine is to inform readers about topics that are of interest to them. E-zines are niche-oriented and therefore are a great way to reach your target market with a very specific message. E-zines also help to position you as a leader in your field.

One of the first questions you might ask is: what is the difference between an e-zine and a blog? An e-zine is e-mailed directly to the recipient's e-mail inbox. Readers do not have to seek the e-zine out like they would with a Web site or pull updates from it as they would with a blog (using an RSS feed). Instead, the e-zine goes to them. E-zines that work well for attracting new clients usually have several key ingredients regarding their content and delivery:

- A memorable name that defines the topic
- A consistency with your brand
- A defined audience and a clear purpose
- A compelling headline or subject line
- Valuable information readers can use
- CAN-SPAM compliance and a privacy statement

(see Sample Opt-In Letter for an E-Zine, page 131)

If the thought of starting your own e-zine is not appealing to you or you do not have time to invest in one, don't worry. There are other ways to get involved, such as writing articles and submitting them to an e-zine that relates to your

SAMPLE OPT-IN LETTER FOR AN E-ZINE OR E-NEWSLETTER

[DATE]

[RETURN ADDRESS]

To Our Clients, Readers and Friends of the Firm:

As an ongoing effort to bring valuable news and information to our clients and constituents, we have added an electronic version of our complimentary quarterly newsletter, [TITLE HERE]. With our next issue scheduled for publication in [MONTH, YEAR], we are pleased to offer you the option of receiving an electronic version of our newsletter.

If you and anyone else in your organization would like to receive this newsletter by e-mail, please complete the information below and return it to our office by mail at the address above, by fax to [FAX NUMBER HERE] or by e-mailing the information to [E-MAIL ADDRESS HERE].

Your Name: _____ Title:_____
Organization: _____
Street/P.O. Box Address:_____
City: _____ State:_____ ZIP: _____
E-mail Address: _____

Other individuals in your organization to be added to our electronic mailing list:

Name: _____ Title:_____
E-mail Address: _____
Name: _____ Title:_____
E-mail Address: _____
Name: _____ Title:_____
E-mail Address: _____

☐Please check this box if you do not wish to receive our newsletter by e-mail but prefer to continue receiving it by regular mail in the future.

Sincerely,

[NAME]

niche. Editors of e-zines, much like editors of blogs, are usually open to and interested in receiving articles from outside sources. This is largely due to the fact that many e-zine editors have other full-time jobs, so they are appreciative when they receive quality articles.

If you do decide that an e-zine is the right communication tool for you, here are a few tips to help you stand out from the masses:

- Provide quality content regularly.

- Strive to build relationships.

- Create a persona that's yours alone.

- Allow the readers to contact you with questions or comments.

- Post questions and comments when appropriate and with permission.

- Be yourself and be different.

- Be resourceful.

- Create a prospective subscriber outreach plan.

- Comply with the rules of ethics as they relate to opt-in readership, required language and disclosures.

Virtual Networking: It's Not Cigars and Caviar Anymore

Unlike the Bar function and networking luncheon, virtual networking has a life all its own. There's no need to worry about your physical appearance, you don't have to bring your business cards, and you don't have to prepare your 30-second introduction.

Virtual networking is like speed dating on steroids. You can be at home, on the train, in a bus or on the beach—no one knows, and it really doesn't matter as long as you have a connection to the Internet. With virtual networking, you type information about yourself on one end. Within nanoseconds, it is published on the World Wide Web for anyone to access.

Virtual networking comes in many forms. It can mean a social membership on MySpace, contributing regular dialog to a ListServ or engaging in professional networking through sites such as LinkedIn, Ryze, BizWiz, Twitter or Spoke. Social networking Web sites are also be helpful because they demonstrate who you know, who you may know through affiliation, and who knows someone you might want to know. LinkedIn, Spoke and other similar sites illustrate the "six degrees of separation" concept that everyone is connected by a chain of six people or fewer.

So, think of it this way. You (the attorney) have just received a telephone call that XYZ Company would like you to prepare a proposal to represent them in a brewing matter. You also learn that the CEO, Jennifer Leader, CFO, Miles Black and in-house counsel, Morra Winner, are the decision makers for XYZ Company.

So, as a member of several online business networks, you log in to the first and type in "Jennifer Leader" to see whether she is a member of the same network. Lo and behold, you find that there are just three degrees of separation between you. You then type in "Miles Black" and find out that he is not listed on your network. Finally, you type in "Morra Winner" and learn that she's not only a member, but she's connected to you by one degree of separation through your friend Trudee Gunnar with whom you served on an ABA panel last year. So now you can do one of two things: you can e-mail Trudee through the network and ask her to connect you to Morra Winner (which I would not recommend), or you can call Trudee, tell her you're presenting a proposal to XYZ Company and ask her, if she is comfortable doing so, to make a call to Morra with a personal recommendation. This just took the legwork out of researching the detailed background of each of the decision makers, finding out what boards they serve on, which universities they graduated from, then trying to find someone who may know them. This does not mean that the personal touch is gone. On the contrary, online networks allow us to get to the end result exponentially faster than we would with traditional means.

For additional information on growing your business through virtual networking, you might want to pick up *The Virtual Handshake: Opening Doors and Closing Deals Online,* by David Teten and Scott Allen. This is the first book to discuss how online communities and other social software can be used to connect with the right people to help you advance your career.

Tag, You're It

You can also reach out to your target audiences by providing them with links to information that they might find helpful. Using social bookmarking sites or networks, it is possible to store lists of useful Internet resources. Each favorite is "tagged" with a keyword or words.

To create a collection of social bookmarks, you would register with a social bookmarking site, which lets you store bookmarks, add tags of your choice, and designate individual bookmarks as public or private. These sites include del.icio.us, Ma.gnolia, reddit, Digg, Google Bookmarks, Yahoo MyWeb and many others.

Some sites periodically verify that bookmarks still work and notify users when a URL no longer functions. Visitors to social bookmarking sites can search for resources by keyword, person, or popularity and see the public bookmarks, tags and classification schemes that registered users have created and saved.

In some cases, your lists can be made accessible to the public. In other cases, they can remain private. When made public, other users with similar interests can view the links by topic, category, tags or even randomly. This is yet another extension of the intricate web of social networking online and how we're becoming a globally connected community.

Craiging from San Francisco to South Africa

Craigslist.org is a free local community of classified advertisements and Internet forums in a relatively noncommercial environment. This popular chain of Web sites started in San Francisco in 1995 and now boasts more than 5 billion page views per month. With 15 million users as of September 2007, the site ranks number seven in use, trailing only Yahoo!, AOL, Microsoft, Google, eBay, and

News Corp. Postings are divided by state, city, country, and many other topics. So, let's "Craig" (yes, that's now a verb). Here's how you can put Craigslist to work for you:

- Include calendar listings for special events.

- Post a listing of your speaking engagements with a head shot.

- Invite the community to your firm or company's open house.

- Post job openings at your firm.

- Announce new hires, promotions and industry awards.

- Post calls for awards applicants.

Most postings on Craigslist have a short lifespan—about one month. So if you want to maintain visibility on the site, be sure to post often and update your previous posts regularly.

However, do not post the same listing in more than one city, or you'll be banned from the list. As an alternative, rewrite your posting with information and an angle that is relevant to a different city. Then post it, but be careful when doing so.

You can keep track of your postings by creating a free user account on Craigslist. By logging in and checking your chart, you will be able to determine which posts have expired and need to be reposted.

As with all of your law firm communications, make sure that whatever you post on Craigslist complies with your state's ethics rules.

Changing at the Speed of Light

Moving forward in time, we're going to see the social networks that we discussed earlier providing a platform for blogs within their networks. This is already available with Twitter and Yahoo! 360°, among others—yet another shift in Web 2.0.

Every day, there is something new to be learned about the use of electronic communications. There are new resources, social media outlets, directory listings, blogs, e-zines and other tools. The time has come for communicators and lawyers alike to embrace social media, to learn how to use it strategically, and to not throw caution to the wind when it comes to communicating within the bounds of legal ethics.

As Web 2.0 takes deep root in mainstream media, it's time to employ it early and often in your everyday public relations efforts.

CHAPTER ELEVEN

" It is not easy to describe the present position
of legal opinion on advertising and free speech.
Only a poet can capture the essence of chaos. "
—*R. H. Coase,*
Advertising and Free Speech, 1977

How to Comply
When You
Communicate

I wish I could say that everything I ever needed to know
about legal communications and the governing rules of
ethics I learned in law school. But that's nowhere near
the truth. As a matter of fact, I do not remember the
Pennsylvania or New Jersey Bar exams asking questions like: "Assuming you've passed the Bar exam, can
you call yourself a legal expert in your attorney biography? Yes or No?"

Accordingly, there was no question asking, "Client tes-
timonials used on your firm's Web site are considered
A) a comparison of one attorney's services to another,
B) false or misleading, C) attorney advertising, or D)
none of the above." Back then, I probably would have
picked, D, none of the above. Ah, but this may not be
accurate either—at least not in some states.

William E. Hornsby, staff counsel for the American Bar Association (ABA) Division for Legal Services, is the person I usually defer to when I have a question regarding the ethics of legal communications. In my opinion, he is the leading U.S. expert (I'm being careful here; I can say this, but he can't.) in this area of the law. If I'm to do this subject any justice, I must absolutely refer you to Mr. Hornsby's book, *Marketing and Legal Ethics, Third Edition: The Boundaries of Promoting Legal Services,* which you can purchase through the ABA Web site. You can also find current developments and updates regarding state rules and ethics opinions at www.abanet.org/cpr/professionalism/lawyer-ad.html.

My own personal disclaimer is that this chapter is not intended to cover the ethics and legal communications rules of every state. It is meant to serve as a resource—a general guide, if you will—so that you can take all the steps necessary to comply when you communicate.

A Brief History of the Model Rules

As we all know, the rules of professional conduct vary widely from state to state. Beginning in 1908, we had the Canons of Professional Ethics, which were last amended in 1963. Then in 1969, the ABA gave us the first Model Code of Professional Responsibility. In 1983, the ABA adopted its Model Rules of Professional Conduct, which were intended to serve as a springboard for state rules across the country. In 1997, the ABA revisited the Model Rules, making yet more changes. Finally, in 2002, the ABA adopted changes that were intended to be more marketing-friendly.

But we can't stop there, because states across the U.S. are continually updating their ethics rules, and many of them are adopting more restrictive and conservative views than those of the ABA.

In the last several years, extremely restrictive rules have been adopted in Connecticut, Florida, Kansas, New Jersey, New York and Washington, D.C., with yet more states to follow. It certainly makes sense that states are revisiting their rules—especially in light of ever-evolving means of electronic communication. With increasing global commerce, electronic marketing tools and Web 2.0, it seems that the only constant will continue to be change.

HOW TO COMPLY WHEN YOU COMMUNICATE

Why the Rules Matter to You and Your Firm

As you have probably noticed, many firms take major risks with their marketing efforts, knowing full well that they may never be called to the table. There are not many states that have the ability to police legal advertising effectively. However, it's more prudent to play within the rules than to risk being sidelined by an ethics violation.

There are several problems that you can run into if you don't comply. They include:

A disciplinary claim against you: It just takes one person to file a complaint against you, subjecting you to disciplinary proceedings. In many states, even the slightest admonishment is open to the public, which obviously isn't good for business. The process is no different than if a client reported your firm for suspected comingling of funds. It's no fun. Some firms choose not to concern themselves with compliance. That's a risk that I wouldn't be willing to take.

Wasted time and money: Law firms today spend a substantial amount of money on their communications. From business-development programs to Web sites and media relations, law firms are shelling out major funds to gain a competitive edge. Playing within the rules ensures that your investments are secure. Just imagine having your firm's tagline or logo deemed misleading after you've rolled out a Web site; issued new business cards, letterhead and envelopes; printed brochures; and sent out other communications featuring your brand identity. The money and time that it would cost to fix the mistake are well worth the upfront investment to ensure compliance.

Increased exposure to malpractice claims: In most cases, your firm's advertising will not create a direct link to potential malpractice claims. However, when the firm's communications include language that may be construed as increasing a client's expectations of a certain outcome, and that outcome is not achieved, the client may have a leg to stand on in a malpractice suit.

What You Absolutely Must Do to Comply

Here is a checklist of things that you absolutely must do to comply when you communicate. It is important to remember that this is a general checklist. You must, and I repeat, MUST, comply with the rules in EVERY state in which you market, have an office and/or seek clients.

☐ Institute internal policies and procedures for all advertising, marketing, public relations and business development materials.

☐ Develop internal compliance procedures.

☐ Stay up to date on all the rules that affect you, your firm and your communications efforts.

☐ Follow the rules in every state in which you market, have an office, have attorneys licensed to practice and/or seek clients.

☐ Include a disclaimer with the language required by each state where you conduct or seek business.

☐ If you think it sounds false or misleading, then assume it is.

☐ If your mother would have a specific expectation as a result of your communication, then so will others.

☐ Include all the facts without omitting anything that provides clarity.

☐ Do not compare one lawyer or law firm to another.

☐ Steer clear of subjective claims *(see Rubel's List, page 141)*.

☐ Do not use language that may create an unjustified expectation.

☐ Reach out to your Bar Association for an opinion when you are in doubt.

☐ Create a system for keeping copies of all communications and for storing them for years to come. State on your Web site in your disclaimer that information on your Web site is "void where prohibited."

RUBEL'S LIST OF SUBJECTIVE CLAIMS

• Able	• Greater
• Advanced	• Highly Qualified
• Aggressive	• Intelligent
• Better	• Proficient
• Bigger	• Proven
• Competent	• Qualified
• Established	• Skilled
• Experienced	• Smart
• Expert	• Super
• Expertise	• Superior

Common Mistakes to Avoid

There are many ethical mistakes, and they vary greatly from state to state. Some of the more common ethical marketing mistakes include:

- Failure to maintain a record of your communications for a specified number of years;

- Calling yourself an "expert" in written materials such as press releases and pitches;

- Making a false statement about the firm's previous successes, such as "We always get the results our clients desire;"

- Not including required language on written and electronic communications;

- Creating an unjustified expectation, such as "We will get money for you";

- Soliciting work the firm refers out. For example, encouraging your audience to "call if you've been arrested for drunk driving," when the firm actually sends all DUI cases elsewhere;

- Making subjective statements about the quality of the firm's work, such as "the best intellectual property law firm in the city";

- Omitting required disclaimers and failing to include any and all statements of limitations.

LEGAL MARKETING ETHICS RESOURCES

- ABA/BNA Lawyers' Manual on Professional Conduct
- Abanet.org
- Aprl.net
- Law.cornell.edu/ethics
- Legalethics.com
- Lfmi.com
- "Marketing and Legal Ethics, Third Edition: The Boundaries of Promoting Legal Services," by William E. Hornsby

It's All Grey

Under many states' rules, there are still numerous grey areas when it comes to legal communications. Blogs, instant and text messages, metatags, search engine advertisements, the use of social media, chat rooms, forums, tags and wikis typically are not addressed by rules of ethics or ethics opinions. On the other hand, some states, such as New York, include all electronic communications, from Web sites to instant messages, in their definitions of marketing.

Task forces are popping up across the U.S. through statewide Bar Associations to review current rules and offer recommendations. Their goals are similar: to limit attorney communications that might hurt the profession and affect the public's perception of lawyers.

HOW TO COMPLY WHEN YOU COMMUNICATE

142

Of course, what constitutes "good taste" is just as subjective as calling an attorney an expert, isn't it?

The Future of the Rules

The ethics of legal communications remains a complex, controversial and ever-evolving maze grounded in the First Amendment's free speech guarantee.

There is a growing trend toward antitrust actions challenging various states' rules. In New York, the Federal Trade Commission (FTC) addressed the most recent Bar Association recommendations by saying that advertising and solicitation restrictions "should be specifically tailored to prevent deceptive claims and should not unnecessarily restrict the dissemination of truthful and nonmisleading information."

Unfortunately for attorneys and legal marketers alike, there are no easy answers. Lawyer marketing generates fervent and logical arguments for and against current restrictions.

Pennsylvania attorney Thomas Cooper put it best in his article, "The Wolf by the Ears: The PBA Copes with Lawyer Advertising," which was published in *The Pennsylvania Bar Association Quarterly* (July 2007, Volume LXXVIII, No.3).

He said, "Lawyers' willingness to indulge some forms of advertising and client solicitation, while opposing other forms of solicitation that they regard as lowly and degrading, creates a dichotomy that makes it difficult for a Bar organization to fashion generic and workable rules that can be applied evenhandedly across the board."

This is so true!

CHAPTER TWELVE

As is the case in all branches of art, success depends in a very large measure upon individual initiative and exertion and cannot be achieved except by dint of hard work.

—Anna Pavlova
Advertising and Free Speech, 1977

Measuring Your Objectives

So now that you have set "measurable" public relations objectives for your law firm and executed tactics to reach your target audiences, you need to measure the success of your public relations plan. The chapter will help you to become familiar with the tools that you will use to assess the success of your public relations. Think in terms of coverage, exposure, reach, placement, demand, impact, calls, leads generated and new business. Before you do anything, you need to define the measurement metrics that are right for you. The bottom line is that the metrics you choose must support your goals, and your goals must define the metrics you use.

First, ask and answer the following questions:

- Have we succeeded in achieving our goals?

- What has happened as a result of our public relations program?

- How can we improve our public relations programs in the future?

- How are we going to track the success of our public relations efforts?

Public relations measurement and evaluation is essential for determining the effectiveness or value of a strategic plan or effort. It remains the most discussed, evolving and challenging issue in the PR industry.

In the short term, PR measurement and evaluation involves assessing the success or failure of programs, strategies, activities or tactics by measuring the outputs, outtakes and/or outcomes against a predetermined set of objectives. In the long term, PR measurement and evaluation involves assessing the success or failure of much broader efforts that were formulated to improve and enhance the relationships that attorneys and their firms maintain with key constituents.

There is no all-encompassing research tool or technique that can be relied upon to measure and evaluate public relations effectiveness. Measuring media content, for example, can give insight into how much exposure your messages received, but it cannot by itself measure whether target audiences actually saw the messages and responded to them in any way. So whether you plan to go it alone or hire a measurement firm to assist with the evaluation of your public relations efforts, you must track the outcomes and effectiveness of your communications.

Tracking Business to Its Origins
With the pressure to be competitive and retain and acquire more clients, law firms know that they must thoroughly execute their communications plans. But few take the time to learn where their business comes from. How do you know for certain that 35 percent of your new cases came from referrals, or that the seminar you hosted didn't result in any new clients? If you don't ask where every lead comes from, you are only doing half the job.

Consider what happens when a prospect calls your firm. The receptionist decides who will get the call. Maybe there is a conversation or a voicemail message. But the prospect does not become a client. Maybe the e-mail was deleted or the pink message slip tossed. No one knows how that prospect learned about the firm. If the prospect was referred by another attorney and that attorney is not thanked, you may lose future referrals from that source.

But what if your receptionist asked how the caller heard about your firm and recorded the response in a database or journal? What if you found out that your firm actually received 10 calls from your most recent seminar, but none were converted into clients? Then you could re-evaluate your marketing efforts. Instead of asking why your seminar didn't generate leads, you would focus on why those 10 prospects weren't converted into clients. Did you target the proper market? If so, was there a failure somewhere between intake and closing the deal with the potential client? Follow up with the lead and find out.

Or let's suppose that plenty of people attended your seminar, but no prospects called your firm afterward. If your audience was well defined and your messages were on target, why did the seminar fail to make an impact? Did you ask attendees to review the seminar? If so, the answer may lie in their evaluations. If not, put your evaluation, tracking and measurement programs in place in order to determine the value of your programs. If your seminars don't result in leads, maybe seminars are not the best way to reach your target after all.

As you can see, failing to measure your results could leave you wasting money when you create and implement future marketing plans. Think of skipping this step as writing a brief without Shepardizing the case law: You had good intentions and strong plans but bad results. Your arguments are worthless if the Supreme Court recently overturned your lead case. Likewise, your marketing plan is only of value when you track, measure and evaluate its effectiveness.

Public Relations Measurement Lingo

To measure both the short- and long-term success of your public relations program, you need to be familiar with basic public relations measurement techniques, tools and terms. This will help you choose the most effective measurements for your business situation. You should, however, know that it is often easier and more reliable (but much more costly) to hire a measurement firm to provide you with the information you need. Also note that there is an excellent blog maintained by K.D. Paine at kdpaine.blogs.com/themeasurementstandard/, which I highly recommend to anyone planning to execute and measure their own public relations strategies.

PUBLIC RELATIONS MEASUREMENT AND MONITORING RESOURCES

There are numerous options for measuring and monitoring your public relations campaigns. Some services focus on one form of media only, such as radio, television, print or social media. Others provide more comprehensive services. Included in this list are a number of resources that are currently available to help you monitor and measure your public relations campaigns.

- BurrellesLuce: Print Clipping Service (Burrellesluce.com)
- Cision: Media Monitoring and Measurement Data (Cision.com)
- Context Analytics: Contextualize Measurement Data (Context-analytics.com)
- Coremetrics: Web 2.0 Metrics (Coremetrics.com)
- Critical Mention: Broadcast Search and Monitoring Data (Criticalmention.com)
- Cymfony, a division of TNS Media Intelligence: Social and Traditional Media Analytics (Cymfony.com)
- DNA13: Media Monitoring and Measuring Service (Dna13.com)
- eNR Services: Media Monitoring Service (Enewsrelease.com)
- Metrica: Media Analysis (Metrica.net)
- National Aircheck: Radio Monitoring (National-aircheck.com)
- Nielson: Television and Radio Measurement (Nielsonmedia.com)
- PR Newswire: Print and Online Measurement (Prnewswire.com)
- Radian6: Social Media Monitoring (Radian6.com)
- RelevantNoise: Blog and Social Media Data (Relevantnoise.com)
- SnapStream: Television Monitoring Service (Snapstream.com)
- VMS: Video Monitoring Service (Vidmon.com)
- Vocus: Traditional and Social Media Monitoring and Measurement Software (Vocus.com)

Whether you engage a professional media measurement firm or try to do it yourself, here is the lingo that you need to know:

Awareness (a.k.a. Message Impact): Awareness or message impact measures awareness, attitude and behavior changes that may have resulted from your PR efforts. This is usually measured via surveys or focus groups but can be gauged through general feedback received from public relations programs if your budget is limited. Comparative studies are required to determine whether there have been any changes in audience awareness and comprehension levels. This can be accomplished through before-and-after quantitative surveys, test and control group studies, focus groups, qualitative depth attitude surveys of target audience groups, and other multivariant studies that rely on observation, participation and attitudinal evaluation.

Comparative Ad Equivalency: The most controversial of all PR measurement tools, comparative ad equivalency, or "value for placement," measures the financial value of the media coverage you received as a result of your public relations campaign. It literally compares what it would have cost to advertise in the same media space, whether it is print, broadcast or online. It should be noted that many public relations practitioners also believe that the actual value is much greater than the advertising cost because the credibility is much higher when the story appears as news, as opposed to paid advertising. Leaders in the PR industry also encourage practitioners to use "audited data," which is the average cost of a media purchase, as opposed to "rate card data." One source for such information is www.sqad.com.

Competitive Analysis: For trade publicity, competitive analysis is very valuable. Review all articles in your target publications to measure the amount of coverage you have garnered vs. your competitors during the relevant time period prior to your public relations efforts. Contrast current levels of coverage with this measurement to demonstrate the heightened coverage your firm has attained due to your public relations efforts.

Leads Generated: Leads generated calculates the number of new client leads produced as a result of your public relations campaign through the attendance or participation in your public relations programs and through proactive demand for your firm's services.

Media Content Analysis: Media content analysis studies, tracks and analyzes the content of your public relations messages as they appear in print, television, radio and Internet communications. The prime function of media content analysis is to determine whether your key messages, concepts and themes were disseminated to others via the media. The variables considered in this analysis include the medium, the placement of your message, the mention of the attorney's or firm's name, the subject of the placement and the subjective value of the overall piece.

Media Coverage: Media coverage measures the number of successful placements and the type of media within which the clips are found.

Media Demand: Media demand is determined by whether the media proactively responded to the press materials that you supplied. Did reporters call? Did you land interviews? Did the TV cameras roll? Over time, do the media reach out to you or your firm's attorneys as a source for quotes?

Media Mapping: Media mapping visually demonstrates local, regional or national media placements. Create a map of the United States and use "dots" or other markers to indicate where placements have appeared. This can visually demonstrate a large number of placements overall (many dots) or a well-controlled regional placement in a localized campaign (clustered dots).

Media Reach (a.k.a. Media Exposure): The reach measures the number of people receiving the communication via the media, also known as the number of media impressions. In order to calculate print reach, determine circulation numbers for all of the publications carrying your messages. This is the raw number of subscribers who were exposed to the story. Multiply print circulation numbers by a "pass-along" factor of 2.5 to determine the number of readers potentially exposed to your story. Broadcast reach is determined by the number of viewers (rating) at the particular time of day that your story aired. Radio reach is determined by the number of listeners. Online reach is determined by the number of unique and repeat visits as measured by tracking software.

Relationship Analysis: As partnerships and joint campaigns are effective public relations approaches, measuring the value of relationships that are built or strengthened through a campaign is a new challenge. Because the relationships are long-lasting and have potential for future benefit and collaborations, their value goes beyond traditional publicity measures. Simple measures of immediate relationship value include event attendance, membership figures, newsletter readership and analysis of each partner's links to other influential companies, organizations, bloggers and the like.

Return on Investment (ROI): ROI is traditionally associated with marketing and advertising tactics; however, we are seeing ROI discussions pop up more and more in public relations. ROI is a financial term that determines the incremental gain divided by the cost. Therefore, ROI equals the incremental gain in business divided by the invested resources multiplied by 100 percent.

Share of Voice/Share of Discussion: Share of voice or SOV (a.k.a. Share of Discussion or SOD), is the percentage one company has of the total amount of communication directed to a targeted group. Good SOV is considered a contributing factor to successful awareness campaigns. This captures and compares your firm's positive and neutral media coverage to that of your competitors and takes into consideration the media value and tone of the coverage. This measurement also subtracts the value of negative stories, which determines the "Net Favorable Media Cost of Impressions" (NFMCI). The NFMCI is then divided by the total of all competitors to obtain the SOV/SOD percentage score. If this sounds cumbersome, it is. The good news is that there are many measurement services that can help you with these determinations.

Assessing the success or failure of specific public relations programs, strategies and activities and their impact upon improving and enhancing your relationships with key audiences is an important discipline. It's also important to understand that measurement programs must evolve just as quickly as communications vehicles. While we have focused on user visits to our Web sites and blogs during the last decade, we are now shifting to user engagement (i.e. what the visitors' behavior looks like). Staying on top of these trends will be important as you evaluate the success of your communications.

So now that you've read the book, what are you going to do about your public relations plan? It's time to sit down execute the plan to build your sustainable home.

Go back and review your corporate business goals. Then review the eight steps from Chapter 2 in order to develop your measurable and sustainable public relations plan. The answers to the following eight-step questions will result in the creation of your public relations plan.

1. What are you goals and objectives?

2. How you want to be perceived?

3. Who are your target audiences?

4. What are your key messages?

5. What do you want your target audiences to do?

6. Which tactics will persuade your target audiences to act in the desired manner?

MEASURING YOUR OBJECTIVES

7. Which tactics are you going to implement to generate optimal results?

8. How are you going to measure your successes against your goals and objectives?

If you follow the formula set out in this book, you should have no problem achieving positive and lasting outcomes with your everyday public relations.

There are a myriad of public relations and marketing resources available. Some of my favorites are listed here.

American Bar Association

www.abanet.org
The American Bar Association (ABA) is the largest voluntary professional association in the world. Many resources can be found on the ABA's Web site that deal with the ethics of legal communications.

American Legal Ethics Library

www.law.cornell.edu/ethics
The American Legal Ethics Library provides access to a digital library containing codes or rules that set standards for the conduct of lawyers.

Association of Professional Responsibility Lawyers

www.aprl.net
The Association of Professional Responsibility Lawyers provides a national clearinghouse of information regarding recent developments and emerging issues in the areas of admission to practice law, professional ethics, disciplinary standards and procedures, and professional liability.

Do-It-Yourself Public Relations:
A Success Guide for Lawyers

This book, published by the ABA's Law Practice Management Section and authored by David E. Gumpert, offers great tips, tools, tactics and practical suggestions for implementing good media relations. The book is available for purchase through the ABA Web site.

Free Publicity
www.publicityinsider.com
Free Publicity is a subscription-only newsletter that features tips, leads, resources and expert advice. As a matter of fact, I author the monthly "Rubel's Rolodex," and here's what the publisher, Bill Stoller, has to say about it: "Every month, top PR Expert Gina Rubel opens up her private 'black book' of media contacts exclusively for subscribers only! This prized info would take you an entire career to compile!"

LegalEthics.com
www.legalethics.com
The LegalEthics Web site contains online resources to legal ethics opinions and law throughout the United States.

Legal Marketing Association (LMA)
www.legalmarketing.org
The Legal Marketing Association (LMA) is a not-for-profit organization dedicated to serving the needs and maintaining the professional standards of those involved in marketing the legal profession.

O'Dwyer's PR/Marketing Communications
www.odwyerpr.com
O'Dwyer's features breaking news about public relations and marketing communications, commentary, professional development resources, a database of public relations firms and job postings.

Public Relations Society of America
www.prsa.org
The Public Relations Society of America, headquartered in New York City, is the world's largest professional organization for public relations practitioners. This Web site is packed with useful information.

A communications expert, attorney and publicist, Gina F. Rubel, Esq., is the owner of Furia Rubel Communications, Inc., a full-service woman-owned certified public relations agency. With a niche in legal communications, Furia Rubel provides expert strategic planning and public relations programs to service providers, educational institutions, and nonprofit organizations throughout the U.S., the U.K. and Canada.

A graduate of Drexel University and Widener University School of Law, Gina has handled a wide range of legal communications, from internationally publicized death penalty appeals to whistle-blower matters. She also served on a Supreme Court of Pennsylvania Disciplinary Board Hearing Committee for six years, where she conducted attorney ethics reviews.

Since she launched Furia Rubel, Gina's clients have been featured everywhere from MSNBC and "The Today Show" to NPR, *The New York Times* and *The Wall Street Journal*. A client advocate and business diplomat, Gina knows how to apply strategic planning to achieve clients' goals and objectives.

Gina resides in Pennsylvania with her husband and two children on a 250-year-old farm. When she's not working, you will find her spending time with her family gardening, hiking, taking photographs and traveling.

Host an *Everyday Public Relations for Lawyers* Seminar

Law firms nationwide are hosting in-house professional development programs to give their attorneys and legal marketing staff the tools they need to succeed. You can, too.

Host an *Everyday Public Relations for Lawyers* Seminar and be prepared to reap the benefits. Your counsel will walk away with everyday practical tips and a no-nonsense strategic public relations plan.

Stop saying that only 20 percent of your attorneys are rainmakers. Give every lawyer the tools to succeed.

To have Gina conduct an *Everyday Public Relations for Lawyers* Seminar in your workplace, please visit:

www.FuriaRubel.com

To receive relevant, up-to-date information about legal communications and industry trends, subscribe to:

www.ThePRLawyer.com

> Attorneys today rely on marketng and public relations to attract and retain clients. Those who don't, fail to do so at their peril.
> —*Gina Furia Rubel, Esq.*

Everyday Public Relations for Lawyers

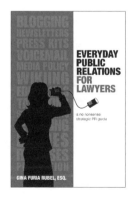

In today's competitive marketplace, attorneys can no longer ignore the power of public relations. This straght forward and practical guide covers everything that seasoned and new lawyers alike need to know about promoting themselves, their law firms and their practices.

Everyday Public Relations for Lawyers provides hands-on advice on all aspects of public relations, from the do's and don'ts of media relations to controlling your message to harnessing the power of the Internet.

To order additional copies of this book, for your colleagues, visit:

www.ThePRLawyer.com